BIRDS

GROUND BIRDS

Ostrich, Pheasants, Turkeys, Bustards ...

ROB HUME

GROLIER

Two of North America's larger species of game bird: common turkey (1); sage grouse (2).

1

2

Published 2003 by Grolier,
Danbury, CT 06816
An imprint of of Scholastic Library Publishing

This edition published exclusively for the school and library market

Planned and produced by
Andromeda Oxford Limited
Kimber House
1 Kimber Road
Abingdon, Oxon OX14 1BZ

www.andromeda.co.uk

Project Director: Graham Bateman
Project Manager: Derek Hall
Editors: Marion Dent, John Woodward
Art Editor and Designer: Tony Truscott
Cartographic Editor: Tim Williams
Editorial Assistants: Marian Dreier, Rita Demetriou

Picture Manager: Claire Turner
Picture Researcher: Vickie Walters
Production: Clive Sparling

Printed in China

Set ISBN 0-7172-5731-2

Library of Congress Cataloging-in-Publication Data

Birds.
    v. cm. — (World of animals ; v. 11-20)
Includes index.
Contents: [1] Ground birds / Rob A. Hume — [2] Seabirds / Jonathan Elphick — [3] Shorebirds / Derek W. Niemann, Euan Dunn — [4] Waterbirds / Tony Whitehead, Derek W. Niemann, David Chandler — [5] Hunting birds / John Woodward — [6] Seed-, fruit-, and nectar-eating birds / Dominic Couzens — [7] Insectivorous birds / Rob A. Hume — [8] Omnivorous birds / Derek W. Niemann, David Chandler, Tony Whitehead — [9] Tropical forest birds / Jonathan Elphick — [10] Unusual birds / Dominic Couzens.
    ISBN 0-7172-5731-2 (set) — ISBN 0-7172-5732-0 (v. 1) — ISBN 0-7172-5733-9 (v. 2) — ISBN 0-7172-5734-7 (v. 3) — ISBN 0-7172-5735-5 (v. 4) — ISBN 0-7172-5736-3 (v. 5) — ISBN 0-7172-5737-1 (v. 6) — ISBN 0-7172-5738-X (v. 7) — ISBN 0-7172-5739-8 (v. 8) — ISBN 0-7172-5740-1 (v. 9) — ISBN 0-7172-5741-X (v. 10)
    1. Birds—Juvenile literature. [1. Birds.] I. Series: World of animals (Danbury, Conn.) ; v. 11-20.
QL676.2.B57 2003
598—dc21
                                                    2003048308

About This Volume

One of the most remarkable attributes of birds is their power of flight, yet some species have dispensed with flying altogether, and others fly only rarely. Such a strategy is risky, since flight is a prime means of escaping ground predators. However, birds that live all or part of their lives on the ground have developed solutions to this problem. Large species like the ostrich are magnificent sprinters and long-distance runners, and can often outrun mammals that might attack them. Others, such as the tinamous and female game birds, have plumage that provides excellent camouflage; they simply crouch stock-still to escape detection. The cassowary can disable attackers with a powerful kick. Bustards and game birds can explode into the air with a sudden burst of flapping wings if threatened and, once airborne, can fly short distances. Ground birds must find sufficient nutritious food within an area that they can cover on foot each day and during all seasons, because they are unable to fly to areas where food is temporarily abundant or migrate to avoid seasonal shortages or extremes of weather. Even so, ostriches and emus in particular cover long distances on foot. Ground birds are highly specialized creatures, unevenly spread over the surface of the globe. Many are highly successful species, well adapted to their chosen habitats; but a few are scarce, like the superb lyrebird, or endangered, like the kagu.

Contents

The kori bustard sometimes provides a mobile perch for smaller species like carmine bee-eaters.

The ratites form a distinct group of flightless birds. Shown below are: emu and chicks (1); ostrich (2); brown kiwi (3).

1

2

3

How to Use This Set

World of Animals: Birds is a 10-volume set that describes in detail birds from all corners of the globe. Each volume brings together those species that share similar characteristics or have similar lifestyles. So birds that spend most of their lives living on the ground are found in Volume 11, seabirds are in volume 12, shorebirds are in Volume 13, and so on. To help you find the volumes containing species that interest you, look at pages 6 to 7 (Find the Animal). A brief introduction to each volume is also given on page 2 (About This Volume).

Article Styles

Each volume contains two types of article. The first kind introduces individual bird families (such as the penguin family) or groups of closely related bird families (such as mockingbirds and accentors). This article reviews the variety of birds in the families as well as their relationship with other bird families and orders. The second type of article makes up most of each volume. It concentrates on describing in detail individual birds typical of the family or families, such as the blue jay. Each such article starts with a fact-filled **data panel** to help you gather information at a glance. Used together, the two styles of article enable you to become familiar with specific birds in the context of their evolutionary history and biological relationships.

Data panel presents basic statistics of each bird

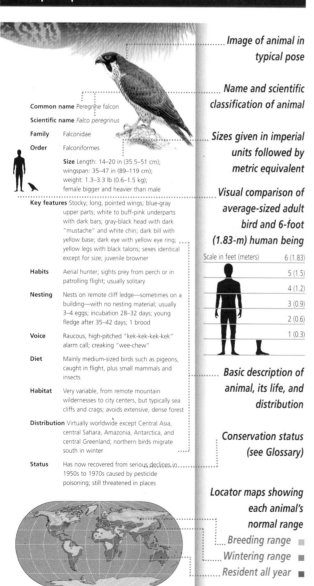

Image of animal in typical pose

Name and scientific classification of animal

Common name Peregrine falcon
Scientific name *Falco peregrinus*
Family Falconidae
Order Falconiformes
Size Length: 14–20 in (35.5–51 cm); wingspan: 35–47 in (89–119 cm); weight: 1.3–3.3 lb (0.6–1.5 kg); female bigger and heavier than male
Key features Stocky; long, pointed wings; blue-gray upper parts; white to buff-pink underparts with dark bars; gray-black head with dark "mustache" and white chin; dark bill with yellow base; dark eye with yellow eye ring; yellow legs with black talons; sexes identical except for size; juvenile browner
Habits Aerial hunter; sights prey from perch or in patrolling flight; usually solitary
Nesting Nests on remote cliff ledge—sometimes on a building—with no nesting material; usually 3–4 eggs; incubation 28–32 days; young fledge after 35–42 days; 1 brood
Voice Raucous, high-pitched "kek-kek-kek-kek" alarm call; creaking "wee-chew"
Diet Mainly medium-sized birds such as pigeons, caught in flight, plus small mammals and insects
Habitat Very variable, from remote mountain wildernesses to city centers, but typically sea cliffs and crags; avoids extensive, dense forest
Distribution Virtually worldwide except Central Asia, central Sahara, Amazonia, Antarctica, and central Greenland; northern birds migrate south in winter
Status Has now recovered from serious declines in 1950s to 1970s caused by pesticide poisoning; still threatened in places

Sizes given in imperial units followed by metric equivalent

Visual comparison of average-sized adult bird and 6-foot (1.83-m) human being

Scale in feet (meters)

	6 (1.83)
	5 (1.5)
	4 (1.2)
	3 (0.9)
	2 (0.6)
	1 (0.3)

Basic description of animal, its life, and distribution

Conservation status (see Glossary)

Locator maps showing each animal's normal range

Breeding range ■
Wintering range ■
Resident all year ■

Article describes a particular bird

Scientific name of animal

Common name of animal

Captions to photographs provide additional information about each animal's lifestyle

OMNIVOROUS BIRDS   *Cyanocitta cristata*
Blue Jay

It is hard to ignore a noisy, confident neighbor, and the vociferous character and audacious habits of the blue jay have earned it an almost iconic status in its native North America.

EVEN THOUGH IT IS ABSENT from the western side of the continent, the blue jay is known throughout North America. Its appearance is certainly memorable. It is strikingly light blue on the top of its head, its wings, back, and tail, with a blue crest at the back of its head. A black eyeline runs into a thick "necklace" that loops around its upper breast. There are fine black bars on its wings, as well as white patches that are highly visible in flight, and it has a long, black-barred tail. It has a voice to match its vivid colors, with an extensive vocabulary ranging from piercing calls to musical whistles.

Essentially, it is a bird of the woodland edge rather than deep forest. In Illinois, for example, its population is higher in towns than in the forests outside. Human settlements offer an attractive alternative to the forests, provided there are enough nut-producing trees available.

ⓘ In winter blue jays rely heavily on nuts and seeds, and they are quick to visit garden bird feeders to gather what they can. Out in the forests they survive by making food caches to see them through the winter.

Common name Blue jay
Scientific name *Cyanocitta cristata*
Family Corvidae
Order Passeriformes
Size Length: 9.5–12 in (24–30 cm); wingspan: 15–16 in (38–41 cm); weight: 2.3–3.8 oz (65–108 g)
Key features Medium-sized, colorful crow, with small crest; blue wings and tail barred with black and white, underparts whitish apart from black "necklace"; black bill and legs
Habits Very bold and noisy; hops rapidly from branch to branch
Nesting Nests made of twigs, moss, grass, and even string in fork or horizontal branch, usually 4–5 eggs; incubation 17–18 days; young fledge after 17–21 days; 1–2 broods
Voice Wide variety of calls, including piercing "jay jay" call and wheedling musical sounds
Diet Fruits, seeds, insects and other invertebrates, small mammals, lizards, nesting birds and eggs, and carrion
Habitat Wooded areas, including forests and parks
Distribution Eastern and central North America
Status Widespread and common, range expanding westward

Cross-references to relevant pages in this and other volumes

94   **SEE ALSO** Crow Family, The **18**:90, Raven, Common **18**:100, Magpie, Eurasian **18**:104

Easy-to-read and comprehensive text

A number of other features help you navigate through the volumes and present you with helpful extra information. At the bottom of many pages are **cross-references** to other articles of interest. They may be to related birds, birds that live in similar places, birds with similar behavior, predators (or prey), and much more. Each volume also contains a **Set Index** to the complete *World of Animals: Birds*. All birds mentioned in the text are indexed by common and scientific names, and many topics are also covered. There is also a **Glossary** that will help you if there are words in the text that you do not fully understand. Each volume includes a list of useful **Further Reading and Websites** that help you take your research further. Under **List of Orders and Families** you will find a complete checklist of all the bird families of the world, highlighting the ones that are featured in the set.

Introductory article describes family or closely related groups

Meticulous drawings illustrate a typical selection of family or group members or supplement text

Tables summarize classification of families and give scientific names of animals mentioned in the text. They also list the total number of genera and species in each family

Graphic full-color photographs bring text to life

At-a-glance boxes cover topics of special interest

Find the Animal

*W*orld of Animals: Birds is the second part of a library that describes all groups of living animals. Each cluster of volumes in *World of Animals* will cover a familiar group of animals—mammals, birds, reptiles, amphibians, fish, and insects and other invertebrates. These groups also represent categories of animals recognized by scientists (see The Animal Kingdom below).

The Animal Kingdom

The living world is divided into five kingdoms, one of which (kingdom Animalia) is the main subject of the *World of Animals*. Kingdom Animalia is divided into numerous major groups called phyla, but only one of them (Chordata) contains those animals that have a backbone. Chordates, or vertebrates, include all the animals familiar to us and those most studied by scientists—mammals, birds, reptiles, amphibians, and fish. There are about 38,000 species of vertebrates, while the phyla that contain animals without backbones (so-called invertebrates, such as insects and spiders) include at least 1 million species, probably many more. To find which set of volumes in the *World of Animals* you need to choose, see the chart The Main Groups of Animals (below).

Birds in Particular

World of Animals: Birds provides a broad survey of some of the most abundant yet unusual and varied creatures that share our planet. Birds are unique in their possession of feathers—a feature that allows the majority of species to fly. Birds are divided into major groups called orders.

Rank	Scientific name	Common name
Phylum	Chordata	Animals with a backbone
Class	Aves	All birds
Order	Charadriiformes	Gulls and their relatives
Family	Sternidae	Terns
Genus	*Sterna*	Sea terns
Species	*caspia*	Caspian tern

The kingdom Animalia is subdivided into phyla, classes, orders, families, genera, and species. Above is the classification of the Caspian tern.

Different orders include birds such as birds of prey, owls, and perching birds. Within each order there are a number of bird families. All the bird orders are shown on the chart on page 7; the common names of some of the most important birds in these orders are also listed. For a comprehensive listing of all the bird families within each order refer to the list on pages 112–113.

Bird classification is a rapidly changing science. Not only have several different ways of grouping birds already been proposed, but new evidence, such as from DNA analysis, has resulted in a major rethinking of the bird family tree; the result is that some species are now placed in different orders or families by different ornithologists. Furthermore, the same bird may have a different scientific or common name according to which classification system is used. Therefore, the system of classification in this set may differ in some respects from others and may itself change as the results of new studies emerge.

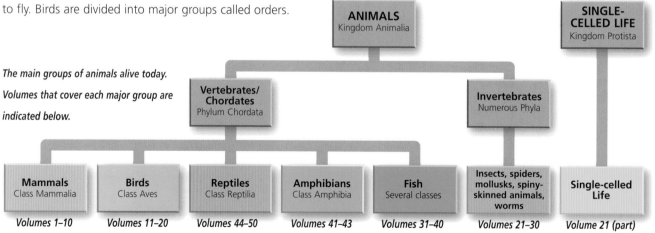

The main groups of animals alive today. Volumes that cover each major group are indicated below.

ANIMALS Kingdom Animalia

SINGLE-CELLED LIFE Kingdom Protista

Vertebrates/Chordates Phylum Chordata

Invertebrates Numerous Phyla

Mammals Class Mammalia	**Birds** Class Aves	**Reptiles** Class Reptilia	**Amphibians** Class Amphibia	**Fish** Several classes	**Insects, spiders, mollusks, spiny-skinned animals, worms**	**Single-celled Life**
Volumes 1–10	*Volumes 11–20*	*Volumes 44–50*	*Volumes 41–43*	*Volumes 31–40*	*Volumes 21–30*	*Volume 21 (part)*

Naming Birds

To discuss animals, names are needed for the different kinds. Most people regard Caspian terns as one kind of bird and Arctic terns as another. All Caspian terns look alike. They breed together and produce young like themselves. This popular distinction corresponds closely to the zoologists' definition of a species. All Caspian terns belong to one species and all Arctic terns to another.

Some animals have different names in different languages or more than one name in a single language. Therefore, zoologists use an internationally recognized system for naming species consisting of two-word scientific names, usually in Latin or Greek. The Caspian tern is called *Sterna caspia* and the Arctic tern *Sterna paradisaea*. The first word, *Sterna*, is the name of the genus (a group of very similar species), which includes the Caspian tern and the Arctic tern. The second word, *caspia* or *paradisaea*, indicates the species within the genus. The same scientific names are recognized the world over. The convention allows for precision and helps avoid confusion. However, a species may have more than one scientific name—it may have been described and named at different times without the zoologists realizing it was one species.

It is often necessary to make statements about larger groups of animals: for example, all the terns or all the birds. Classification makes this possible. Gulls are similar to terns, but less similar than species are to each other. All gull species are placed in the family Laridae, but all gull-like birds, including the tern family, the Sternidae, are placed in the order Charadriiformes. All the bird orders, each containing birds with similarities to each other, are placed in the class Aves (the birds). Finally, the birds are included, with all other animals that have backbones (fish, amphibians, reptiles, and mammals) and some other animals that seem to be related to them, in the phylum Chordata.

The chart shows the likely relationship between groups of birds, although there is disagreement about some of the links. The volume(s) in which each order appears is also indicated. You can find individual entries by looking at the contents page for each volume or by consulting the index.

Ostrich **Order Struthioniformes** *Volume 11*
Emu, cassowaries **Order Casuariiformes** *Volume 11*
Rheas **Order Rheiformes** *Volume 11*
Kiwis **Order Apterygiformes** *Volume 11*
Tinamous **Order Tinamiformes** *Volume 11*

Game birds **Order Galliformes** *Volume 11*

Wildfowl **Order Anseriformes** *Volume 12, 14*

Button quails **Order Gruiformes** *Volume 11*

Honeyguides, jacamars **Order Piciformes** *Volume 17*
Woodpeckers **Order Piciformes** *Volume 18*
Puffbirds, barbets, toucans **Order Piciformes** *Volume 19*

Kingfishers **Order Coraciiformes** *Volume 14*
Rollers **Order Coraciiformes** *Volume 15*
Bee-eaters, hoopoe **Order Coraciiformes** *Volume 17*
Motmots, todies, hornbills **Order Coraciiformes** *Volume 19*
Trogons **Order Trogoniformes** *Volume 19*

Mousebirds **Order Coliiformes** *Volume 20*

Cuckoos, hoatzin **Order Cuculiformes** *Volume 20*

Parrots **Order Psittaciformes** *Volume 16, 19, 20*

Swifts **Order Apodiformes** *Volume 15*
Hummingbirds **Order Apodiformes** *Volume 16*

Owls **Order Strigiformes** *Volume 15*
Nightjars, frogmouths **Order Caprimulgiformes** *Volume 15*
Turacos **Order Cuculiformes** *Volume 16*

Pigeons **Order Columbiformes** *Volume 16*

Bustards, seriemas **Order Gruiformes** *Volume 11*
Cranes, limpkin, rails **Order Gruiformes** *Volume 14*
Trumpeters **Order Gruiformes** *Volume 19*

Pratincoles, coursers **Order Charadriiformes** *Volume 11*
Gulls, terns, auks **Order Charadriiformes** *Volume 12*
Plovers, sandpipers, avocets, oystercatchers, sheathbills
Order Charadriiformes *Volume 13*
Jacanas, painted snipes **Order Charadriiformes** *Volume 14*
Sandgrouse **Order Pteroclidiformes** *Volume 16*

Birds of prey **Order Falconiformes** *Volume 15*
Vultures, secretary bird **Order Falconiformes** *Volume 20*

Grebes **Order Podicipediformes** *Volume 14*

Tropicbirds **Order Pelecaniformes** *Volume 12*

Gannets, cormorants **Order Pelecaniformes** *Volume 12*

Herons, storks, ibises, spoonbills, flamingos
Order Ciconiiformes *Volume 14*
New World vultures **Order Falconiformes** *Volume 20*

Penguins **Order Sphenisciformes** *Volume 12*
Albatrosses, petrels, shearwaters **Order Procellariiformes** *Volume 12*
Pelicans, frigatebirds **Order Pelecaniformes** *Volume 12*
Loons **Order Gaviiformes** *Volume 14*

Perching birds **Order Passeriformes** *Volume 11, 14, 15, 16, 17, 18, 19, 20*

WHAT IS A BIRD?

A bird is a warm-blooded, egg-laying vertebrate (an animal with a backbone) that is typically adapted for flight. It walks on its hind limbs, and its forelimbs are modified to form wings—even in species that cannot fly. A bird has a horny sheath on its jaws that forms a bill, or beak. And most distinctively, a bird has feathers covering most of its body. All living birds are grouped within the class Aves.

Although some other vertebrates—such as bats—can also fly, and a few fish, amphibians, and reptiles can glide through the air, nothing matches birds for sheer aerial ability. Flight has enabled birds to colonize distant lands, invade new habitats, and find food. It has also given them a means of escape from land-bound enemies.

During the course of evolution a few species have lost the ability to fly. Large flightless birds such as the ostrich (*Struthio camelus*) overcome this drawback by virtue of their great size and strength and their ability to outrun their enemies. The wings of penguins have become powerful flippers for propelling the birds through the water instead of through the air.

⊕ *The bird's skeleton is modified for flight. The main flight feathers are attached to the bones of the forelimbs. In cross-section the wing forms an elongated, teardrop shape known as an airfoil, which creates lift as the bird moves through the air. Shown here is a shoveler (Spatula clypeata).*

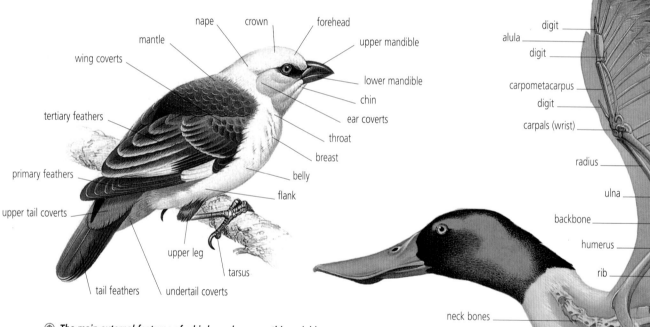

⊕ *The main external features of a bird are shown on this sociable weaver (Philetairus socius).*

Birds (class Aves)
28 orders
181 families
9,600 species (approx.)
All the bird orders are listed on pages 7 and 112–113.
All the bird families can be found on pages 112–113.

The Bird Skeleton

A bird has a backbone consisting of between 40 and 60 vertebrae, depending on the length of its neck. The neck vertebrae allow much more movement than in mammals. Some birds, such as herons, have modified neck bones that produce a sinuous, snakelike appearance—and they also allow the bird to thrust its head and bill forward in a sudden stab. The back vertebrae are often fused together for strength.

The "collarbones" form a V-shaped wishbone, and in most flying birds the breastbone, or sternum, forms a deep keel. The keel provides anchorage for the large pectoral muscles that power the wings in flight. Behind the pelvis the vertebrae form a short, flexible tail.

The wing bones are more elongated than the bones in a mammal's forelimbs. The humerus, or upper arm, is usually short, although in birds with very long wings, such as albatrosses, it is elongated. Typically, the feathers on the inner part of the wing are supported by the radius

⬆ *The bird's digestive system and major internal organs are shown in this jungle fowl (Gallus gallus).*

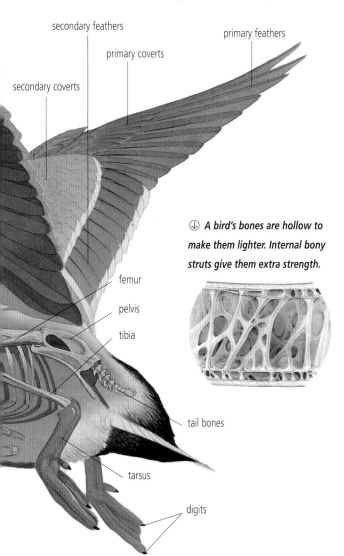

⬇ *A bird's bones are hollow to make them lighter. Internal bony struts give them extra strength.*

The Big and the Small

Birds range in size from the tiny bee hummingbird (*Mellisuga helenae*), which is little bigger than a large insect, to heavyweights like the ostrich, which at 331 lb (150 kg) is the heaviest bird alive and stands taller than a fully grown man. The biggest-known bird, now extinct, was the ostrichlike giant moa (*Dinornis maximus*), which grew to a height of over 10 ft (3 m). The biggest flying birds include bustards, which can weigh over 50 lb (22.5 kg), and albatrosses and condors, with wingspans of 10 ft (3 m) or more.

and ulna, corresponding to the human forearm, while the feathers on the outer half grow from the "hand." The bend of the wing is equivalent to the human wrist.

The thigh bone, or femur, of a bird is usually more or less fixed against the pelvis. The visible upper part of a bird's leg, the fibula and tibia, is equivalent to our "shin." The joint below this is equivalent to the "ankle," which explains why it hinges forward rather than back like a knee joint. The lower part of the leg is the tarsus and

Bird Evolution

The oldest-known bird fossil is still the dinosaurlike *Archaeopteryx*, from the Solnhofen Limestone of the Upper Jurassic of Germany, about 150 million years ago. However, birds belonging to various lineages have also been found in Cretaceous deposits of Asia, Europe, and America. By the close of the Cretaceous, 65 million years ago, a hypothetical birdwatcher would have seen relatives of many of today's familiar birds, such as geese, ducks, gulls, and shorebirds.

Modern birds continued to diversify throughout the Cenozoic. By the early Oligocene, 35 million years ago, most of the bird orders that we recognize today had appeared. Our birdwatcher could have added to the list relatives of today's herons, penguins, crows, vultures, and songbirds. Were he or she birdwatching in South America, however, it would have been best to avoid the phororhachids—flightless, fast-running predatory birds, some nearly 10 feet (3 m) tall and armed with huge beaks and claws. These birds were the dominant South American land carnivores for much of the Cenozoic. Recently, phororhachid bones have also been found in North America and Europe. In the Eocene their niche was occupied by the Diatrymidae. They resembled the phororhachids and probably had a similar lifestyle.

Paleontologist Sankar Chatterjee has recently described the fossil *Protoavis*, from Late Triassic deposits in Texas, about 225 million years ago. He claims that *Protoavis* is closer to modern birds than *Archaeopteryx*. If true, this would push the origin of birds back by about 75 million years. It would also show that the first birds lived at the same time as the earliest dinosaurs—disproving the standard hypothesis that birds are descended from coelurosaurian dinosaurs, which are not known from the Triassic. This would require a major rethink of the evolution of both birds and dinosaurs.

⊕ *The pigeon-sized* **Archaeopteryx** *had reptilian and birdlike features. It possessed claws on all four limbs and jaws armed with teeth, but it had feathers on its body and wings like a bird.*

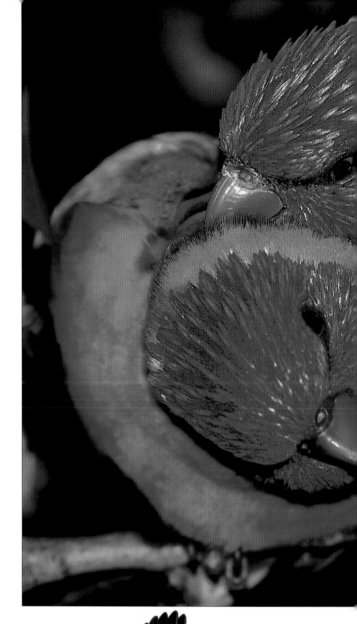

equates to our foot, while the real foot of a bird is made up of the bones that form our toes. The scales on the legs of birds are a clue to their likely reptilian ancestors.

A bird's foot usually has four toes. In many species three point forward and one points back, but some birds, such as woodpeckers, have two toes pointing forward and two back. An owl can turn one toe forward or back to obtain the best grip on prey. Some bird species have only three toes that all point forward; this is typical of birds that run on open ground. Uniquely, the ostrich has only two toes. Birds' toes end in claws, which may be short and blunt or long, thin, and tapered. Birds of prey have strong, curved, very sharp claws for killing and

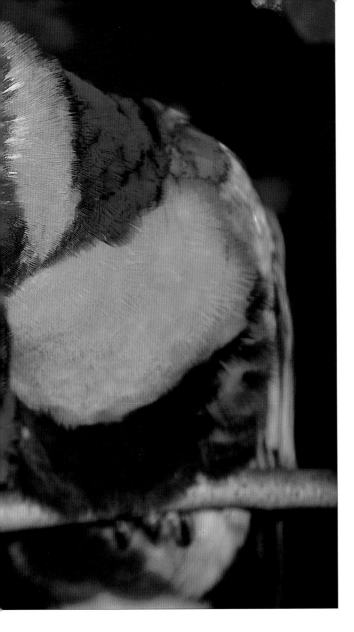

⊖ *Despite their gaudy plumage, parrots such as these preening rainbow lorikeets (Trichoglossus haematodus) still remain remarkably well concealed in their treetop homes.*

help give each species its distinctive shape, color, and pattern. A small bird like a hummingbird has about 900 feathers, whereas a swan may have over 25,000 feathers.

A feather can be colored in two ways. Some feathers are designed to reflect part of the visible wavelength of light in such a way that they appear iridescent. Others have a pigment that gives a "true" color—such as green or red. The commonest feather pigment is melanin.

Feathers are replaced once or twice a year in a process known as molt. Each feather is pushed out as a new one grows beneath it. The molt replaces worn feathers, and the process can also change a bird's color. The black hood of some gulls, for example, becomes white in winter when the black feathers are replaced by white ones. Color can also be changed when dull feather tips wear away in spring to reveal bright colors beneath. Thus the bird acquires a colorful breeding plumage without molting any feathers—saving precious energy late in the winter when food is scarce.

A bird keeps its feathers neat and clean by bathing and preening. It pulls each feather through its bill to remove dirt and parasites and to zip the vanes together. It also treats them with special oil from a preen gland above its tail, perhaps to help waterproofing.

holding prey. Other birds, such as grebes, have broad, flat claws that are almost like fingernails.

Feather Form and Function

A feather is made of keratin—the material that forms our fingernails, as well as the scales of reptiles. A typical large feather has a stiff central shaft that grows from a follicle in the skin, rather like a mammalian hair. Arising from each side of the shaft are barbs, usually longer on one side than the other, that give the feather an aerodynamic shape. Each barb is fringed with tiny hooked barbules that "zip" together to form a broad, flat vane.

There are three main types of feather. Flight feathers are large feathers found on the wings and tail. They are specially strengthened and shaped to provide a smooth surface over which air flows to provide the lift needed for flight. Contour feathers give the bird its streamlined shape. Down feathers form an insulating layer. Feathers

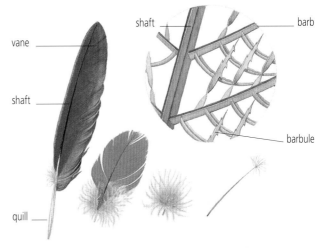

Flight feather   Contour feather   Down feather   Filoplume

⬆ *The hollow shaft and quill support the vane. In closeup (inset) the vane is composed of barbs bearing two rows of barbules. Adjacent barbules lock together, giving the vane rigidity.*

Bird Color and Shape

Although plumage coloration is remarkably constant within individual species, the shape and color of plumage often vary according to sex, season, and age. Males are usually bigger with brighter plumage than females, but this is not always true. Female hawks and falcons are bigger than their mates. Some shorebirds, such as phalaropes, have large, bright females and smaller, dowdy males; in these species the usual roles are reversed, and the male sits on the eggs and raises the young.

Seasonal color differences are common. Most birds flaunt their brightest plumage in spring and early summer, since that is when males court females and defend their territories against other males; colors are important in such activities. Yet most ducks pair up in winter, and it is then that they are at their finest: In summer the males are dull and drab to minimize attracting predators.

Juvenile birds are usually duller than their parents. There are several reasons for this. Some parent birds are very aggressive when nesting, and they chase away other adults anywhere near their nests: It is vitally important that the young birds are not mistaken for intruding adults and attacked. Furthermore, dull colors give young birds better camouflage in the first few weeks of life, when they are inexperienced and vulnerable.

Generally, there is little seasonal change in shape, but some species develop long plumes or tail feathers during the breeding season. More unusually, a puffin develops a large, colorful bill in summer, but sheds the outer sheath in fall so that its bill is small and dull during the winter.

Bills and Feeding

The bird's bill is also a weight-saving device. Birds have lost the heavy teeth and the associated components such as jaws and the muscles used for chewing food. Instead, the bill is formed from bony upper and lower mandibles, capped with a horny sheath. Within this basic structure there is endless variation—nearly always reflecting the bird's food and feeding technique.

Even the tongues of some birds show remarkable adaptations. Some parrots have brushlike tongues for licking nectar from flowers. Woodpeckers have long, pointed, sticky tongues with barbed tips; they coil around the back of the skull when withdrawn but can extend far beyond the tip of the bill to reach inside holes to catch insects. The tongue of flamingos forms a piston for sucking up water containing tiny food particles.

⊕ *Unusually among hornbills, the southern ground-hornbill (*Bucorvus leadbeateri*) is carnivorous. Its bill, shaped like giant forceps, is designed to capture all kinds of prey from insects to amphibians and other small vertebrates.*

Flight Styles

During powered flight strong downward wingbeats provide lift and propulsion. Fast powered flight requires a lot of energy delivered fast. To facilitate this, birds have high body temperatures (in the range of 106–110° F/41–43.5° C) and a high metabolic rate. The flight muscles require large amounts of oxygen, and the lungs are richly endowed with air capillaries. The lungs are also linked to a series of air sacs (right) that penetrate the body spaces. They improve the ability to absorb oxygen and help make the bird lighter.

Flight also involves gliding and soaring, which rely on winds and air currents to provide lift. This type of flight uses the least energy. A vulture or an eagle, for example, uses upcurrents to gain height and stay aloft for hours at

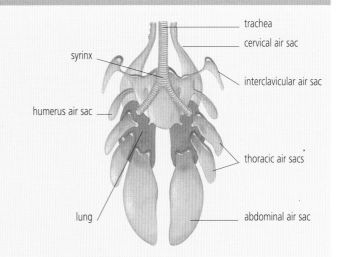

a time with scarcely a flap of its wings. An albatross flies less high, but it uses the wind across the ocean and the air currents over the waves to glide effortlessly for vast distances.

Instead of being chewed, food is swallowed whole and passes into the saclike crop, at the base of the neck, where it is often stored. From there food passes to the muscular gizzard, where it is ground up. Birds do not have a large bladder where urine collects because the weight would impair their ability to fly. Instead, birds' kidneys produce concentrated nitrogenous matter in the form of uric acid. This is voided at the anus along with the feces.

Supersenses

Birds vary in their ability to detect smells. A few, like certain New World vultures, have an excellent sense of smell. Others, such as petrels, probably use smells to find their way to their nests after dark. Most, however, seem to have a poor sense of smell and rely on their ears and their eyes.

Most birds have acute hearing. Thrushes, for example, catch earthworms by listening to their movements underground. Many night-hunting owls rely on sound, and several species have very large ears designed to enable them to locate sound sources with great accuracy in any direction. A great gray owl (*Strix nebulosa*) can even pinpoint small mammals hidden under deep snow by their sound.

A bird's sense of sight is even more highly developed. Many birds—especially eagles, vultures, and their

relatives—are exceptionally gifted. They do not see things larger than we do, but they see more detail and can detect tiny objects at greater distances. A hawk can see a motionless grasshopper on green grass at long range, while we can see nothing but a blur of green. The eyes of owls are equipped with very sensitive retinas that can detect shapes and movements in very low light levels—although they see less detail and probably less color. Pigeons can pick out tiny seeds among similar-looking stones. It is likely that they detect a different wavelength of light reflected by the seeds. In the same way, a hunting kestrel can see the trails of small mammals (and especially their urine and droppings) because they emit different wavelengths of light.

 Like most owls, the eagle owl (Bubo bubo) has large eyes to help gather any available light at night. It also has excellent hearing, although its "ear tufts" are merely feathers that improve camouflage.

Courtship and Breeding

Breeding usually occurs at a time of year when food is abundant for feeding the developing young. Males sport their colorful breeding plumage and usually defend a breeding territory from rival males. Within the territory the birds nest and in due course find food for the young. The territory of a small songbird may be little more than the area immediately around the nest, but for a large bird of prey such as a golden eagle (*Aquila chrysaetos*) it may cover an area of 240 square miles (622 sq km).

⊕ *The chick develops inside a protective waterproof shell. Until it hatches, the chick gets its nourishment from the yolk sac.*

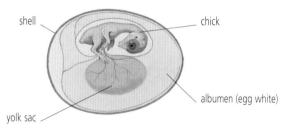

shell   chick

yolk sac   albumen (egg white)

Adult

Nestling

Hatchling

⊕ *Toucans are among the species that produce small, naked, helpless chicks. They are fully dependent on their parents until they grow. Other birds, like ducks, produce chicks that are well developed by the time they hatch and can leave the nest within hours.*

Males then display to attract females. Depending on the species, this can involve singing, showing off the plumage, and adopting various postures. The prenuptial display of some bowerbird species includes males creating colorful "gardens" and bowers to attract the females. Some birds, such as the mute swan (*Cygnus olor*), pair for life. Other species are more promiscuous, and males may mate with more than one female to produce several families each season. Likewise, some females may seek to mate with a variety of males during the breeding season.

Birds usually lay their eggs in nests. They can range from a mere scrape on the ground in some species to the amazingly elaborate, huge hanging nests built by some weaver birds. These nests are often communal structures, with each pair of birds having its own entrance within the overall nest.

For several weeks the chicks develop within their eggs, which are usually kept warm and safe by one or other of the parents gently covering the eggs with its body, a process known as incubation. Some birds are well developed by the time they hatch, but many bird species hatch naked, blind, and helpless. They must be fed and cared for by their parents for weeks, or even months, before they grow full feathers and are ready to leave the nest and feed themselves.

⊕ *Some Eurasian oystercatchers (*Haematopus ostralegus*) are resident, but most migrate between their breeding grounds in Eurasia and their wintering grounds in Africa and further south.*

Bird Migration and Distribution

However skilled a bird is at finding food, at certain times food supplies dry up. When this happens, many birds fly to other parts of the world where food is still plentiful. This seasonal movement is called migration. The Arctic, for example, has vast amounts of insect food available for 24 hours a day in high summer but none at all for the rest of the year. Many birds breed in the Arctic to exploit this abundant summer food supply but retreat south for winter. Other birds make similar movements but do not venture so far north.

Because of the distribution of the continents and the world's weather patterns most bird migration involves species that breed during the northern summer and move southward for the northern winter. There are exceptions within the southern continents, and some seabirds breed in the southern summer and head north to feed in northern oceans in the northern summer. The Arctic tern (*Sterna paradisaea*) does the reverse, breeding in the 24-hour daylight in the Arctic and then spending the winter in almost 24 hours of daylight in the Southern Ocean. It has the longest migratory journeys of any bird and lives in almost perpetual daylight most of the year.

The distribution of a bird means the geographical area in which it is found. That seems straightforward, but it can be a complex issue. A resident species, in which individuals do not move far during the course of their lives, can be mapped quite easily. But many birds migrate; so they have a summer range and a winter range, and there are areas in between where the birds can be seen while on migration. For example, the sanderling (*Calidris alba*) covers vast distances on migration, breeding in the Arctic and wintering as far south as the southern tips of the major landmasses. Therefore its breeding distribution is small, but its overall range is enormous.

Other species have a less regular pattern. Crossbills, waxwings, and nutcrackers periodically irrupt from their breeding ranges in years when their numbers are high but their food supplies are low. In many species that breed far to the north as well as in temperate areas, the northern populations may need to move south in winter to avoid severe weather conditions. But the more southerly populations can stay where they are.

Adaptive Radiation

Some closely related species of birds may live in the same area without competing for food or other essential requirements. They do this because they have evolved slightly differently and so can exploit different resources. This is known as adaptive radiation: Their physical features have "radiated" in several directions from a common ancestor, resulting in different species.

It has long been recognized that two species living close together do not occupy the same niches, but each displaces the other in some way: This is known as competitive exclusion. In North America woodpeckers of similar appearance but different size eat different foods and feed in different parts of a tree. In Europe the various species of titmice have slightly different feeding behavior that allows a mixed flock to feed in the same tree. Shorebirds such as godwits and yellowlegs can all feed in the same estuary because they have different leg and bill lengths, allowing the longer-legged species to wade more deeply and the longer-billed ones to probe more deeply into mud.

Ratites

Struthionidae, Dromaiidae, Casuariidae, Rheidae, Apterygidae

The ratites are flightless, unusual, and mostly very large birds. The group is found across the southern parts of the world from South America (the rheas), through Africa (the ostrich), and into Australia and New Zealand (the emu, cassowaries, and kiwis). In the recent past even more massive flightless birds existed. They included the moas of New Zealand and the gigantic elephant birds of Madagascar—sadly, all now extinct.

A long-running debate has existed about how closely related the ratites really are despite their general similarity in appearance. However, scientists broadly agree that their origins lie in the vast, ancient supercontinent of Gondwanaland that once existed in the Southern Hemisphere. In prehistoric times Gondwanaland split into several parts. The huge landmasses drifted widely across the surface of the Earth, each taking their resident birds, mammals, and other life forms with them. It is thought that a wide-ranging, early ratite ancestor lived on the original supercontinent. After millions of years of separation birds that became isolated on the various landmasses—which eventually became the continents as we know them today—evolved into several new species, including modern-day ratites.

Ratites have well-formed wing bones, but their feathers are weak and poorly developed. Furthermore, the keel (the part of the breastbone to which the flight muscles are attached in flying birds) is also reduced. The mere presence of wings, however, suggests that the creatures may once have been able to fly. Perhaps a lack of large predators meant that flight was unnecessary, and so the keel became reduced. Or perhaps the ratites simply grew larger and larger until flight became impossible for them, and then the keel became smaller because it was no longer required.

Powerful Bodies

Despite the various disagreements and uncertainties, ratites are generally characterized as being round-bodied, short-tailed birds with vestigial wings and loose, silky, bushy feathers. As already mentioned, most ratites are large birds, although the kiwis are much smaller. The larger species have long, powerful legs and strong feet adapted for fast running. The legs are unfeathered and very muscular. The head and bill appear small for the overall size of the bird (although in fact the head is large, with enormous eyes) and are supported on a long, sinuous neck.

The biggest species, the ostrich, ranges in height from 83 to 108 inches (210–275 cm) and weighs between 287 and 331 pounds (130–150 kg). The kiwis, the smallest species, only reach a length of between 14 and 26 inches (36–66 cm) and weigh between 2.2 and 8.4 pounds (1–3.8 kg). Ostriches have just two massive toes per foot. The other big species have three toes, and the kiwis have a tiny fourth hind toe, reduced to little more than a claw.

Family Struthionidae: 1 species	
Struthio	ostrich (*S. camelus*)

Family Dromaiidae: 1 species	
Dromaius	emu (*D. novaehollandiae*)

Family Casuariidae: 1 genus, 3 species	
Casuarius	southern cassowary (*C. casuarius*); one-wattled cassowary (*C. unappendiculatus*); Bennett's cassowary (*C. bennetti*)

Family Rheidae: 2 genera, 2 species	
Rhea	common rhea (*R. americana*)
Pterocnemia	lesser rhea (*P. pennata*)

Family Apterygidae: 1 genus, 3 species	
Apteryx	brown kiwi (*A. australis*); great spotted kiwi (*A. haastii*); little spotted kiwi (*A. owenii*)

→ *Cassowaries, like the one-wattled cassowary shown here, are the largest land animals in New Guinea. Yet glimpses of them are rare, and only their calls, feces, or footprints usually betray their presence.*

Ostriches and rheas have rather flattened bills, but those of emus are deeper and more arched. All ratites, except kiwis, have round, bristly heads with obvious ear openings and almost bare necks. Cassowaries have narrower, curved bills with a flattened, upright, horny casque on top. They also have bare heads with brightly colored skin and wattles and thickly feathered lower necks. Kiwis are quite different. They have a peculiar, short-legged, tailless, squat body, a large head with almost no obvious neck, and wispy bristles around the base of the bill. The bill is long, slim, and tapered, with nostrils at the tip instead of near the base. Unusually among birds, kiwis have an excellent sense of smell.

A Life on the Ground

Several of the ratites live on open plains, where they move around in groups. The groups consist either of family parties or—where the birds are still common—of substantial flocks. Ostriches can still be found traveling in large groups. Not only can ostriches run fast, they are also

⊕ A lesser rhea and chicks grazing in Chile. Rheas resemble ostriches superficially, but there are distinct differences. For example, rheas are smaller and much lighter than ostriches. Rheas also have three toes on each foot, whereas ostriches have only two toes.

Ratite Habitats

The ratites occupy a range of different habitats. The ostrich is an African bird of wide open spaces, where it can run fast and across which it has an excellent view from its high vantage point. Within their range many ostriches live in places where dense thornbush grows, while others are found in near-desert conditions. They tend to avoid long grass that hampers movement and closed woodland that restricts the view.

Rheas are birds of South American plains. They often favor taller grass and scrub at the edge of woodland, usually close to a lake or river. Emus occupy similar places in Australia, but can be seen almost anywhere from forest to semidesert and from undisturbed wilderness to the edges of towns. The cassowaries of New Guinea and northern Australia, however, need rain forest. They prefer undamaged, ancient forest, either flat or hilly, and are unlikely to survive where the forest is disturbed or even selectively felled; wholesale logging spells disaster for them.

Kiwis also prefer rain forest of a more temperate kind, but there is now very little left within their New Zealand range. They have been forced to live in plantations and on bushy slopes where conditions are barely adequate in most places. They seem to prefer a humid climate but can be found from sea level to high peaks at 3,900 feet (1,190 m).

① *Like all kiwis, the great spotted kiwi of South Island, New Zealand, is active at night and hides away in a burrow by day. Even when they emerge, kiwis are hard to see, since they keep to dense undergrowth.*

able to keep going for long distances if necessary. They use their keen eyesight to keep a watch for predators such as lions. They also need to see other ostriches from a distance in order to find and court potential mates. If threatened, ostriches run, but rheas may suddenly flatten themselves against the ground to avoid being spotted.

Ostriches are active by day and may travel great distances—especially when food is hard to find. They are at their most active early and late in the day, but can tolerate extremely hot conditions and are able to move around in the heat of the tropical sun without any ill effects. Rheas sometimes avoid the worst of the heat and feed at night. Emus also seek shade and drink regularly around midday.

Ostriches roost at night in loose groups, usually within sight of several others and positioned so that they are downwind of the direction from which predators would be likely to approach. In a group dominant adults decide on the activity—such as feeding, bathing, drinking, or moving on—and subordinate birds copy the activities of their superiors.

Cassowaries are extremely shy and elusive and live solitary lives except when breeding. They feed in the morning and evening, and also at night when there is sufficient moonlight. They usually rest by day, often seeking a sunny spot close to dense cover. Breeding cassowaries can be remarkably aggressive. They have a massive, sharp claw on each foot and can prove to be deadly foes if attacked.

Kiwis are quite unlike other ratites, being active almost entirely during the hours of darkness. They generally spend the night feeding in dense cover, snuffling around in fallen leaf litter for worms and other small prey.

Tree-climbing Ancestor?

Adult ratites have two, or three, toes that all point forward. Most other birds also have another toe that points backward. This is called an "opposing toe," and it allows the foot to grasp a perch. Ratites cannot grip with their toes, nor do they need to, since they run and walk on open ground and seldom climb higher than the top of an earth mound. Their feet are designed for power and efficiency on the ground. While still in the egg, the embryo of the emu has a backward-facing hind toe, but it turns forward before the chick hatches. It is, however, seen as evidence that the emu's ancestors probably lived in trees.

Common name
Ostrich

Scientific name
Struthio camelus

Family   Struthionidae

Order   Struthioniformes

Size Height:
male 83–108 in
(210–275 cm),
female 69–75 in
(175–190 cm);
weight: male 287–331 lb (130–150 kg),
female 198–243 lb (90–110 kg)

Key features Bare head, neck, and legs; short, flat bill;
large, dark eyes; male black with short, white
wings and tail; female dull gray-brown

Habits   Lives in small groups or flocks, feeding by day

Nesting   Nest a scrape in the ground; usually 7 eggs;
male and dominant female incubate eggs,
including many laid by other females; chicks
gather in large congregations, several families
looked after by 1 pair of adults; young fully
grown at 18 months; mature at 3–4 years;
1 brood

Voice   Variety of short, hard calls, sneezing sounds,
and a loud, deep, roaring or booming sound
from territorial male

Diet   Succulent plants, leaves, buds, seeds, fruits;
rarely insects, small mammals, and reptiles

Habitat   Open spaces from semiarid areas on desert
edge to clearings in savanna woodland;
mostly on open, grassy plains

Distribution Africa south of the Sahara Desert

Status   Rare and threatened in the north and south
of its range; secure in East Africa; some
escaped populations from farmed stock in
southern Africa

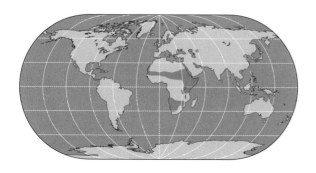

Ostrich

Struthio camelus

*The biggest living bird in the world, the ostrich breaks
all avian records for height, weight, running speed,
and power. Perhaps unsurprisingly, the ostrich also
lays the largest egg of any bird.*

A FEMALE OSTRICH IS THE height of a tall human,
while a male towers over even the tallest of
humans. Old males have dense, black-and-
white plumage on the body, wings, and tail.
There are four races of ostrich: the Masai
ostrich and North African ostrich are
characterized by orange or reddish-pink skin
on their necks, head, and legs, whereas in the
Somali ostrich and South African ostrich the
skin is blue. When breeding, blue-skinned males
have vivid pink bills and shiny pink shins.
Outside the breeding season the skin colors are
much duller. Females, apart from being smaller,
are browner and often look rather dowdy.
Juveniles are drabber and much more unkempt.

Split Distribution

The present range of the ostrich is split into two
areas. The northerly one stretches from the
west coast of Africa across the southern edge
of the Sahara Desert to Somalia and the Horn
of Africa and south into East Africa in the great
game parks of Kenya and Tanzania. The
southern population is found in southwest
Africa. Many ostriches survive in arid regions
like the Sahara and the Kalahari Deserts. Others
are found in much greener landscapes, with
thornbush scrub and acacia woodland, provided
there are grassy clearings and plenty of open
spaces. Ostriches also thrive in quite hilly places,
such as stony slopes with scattered bushes.

Opportunist Feeders

Ostriches eat almost anything edible they can
find, but by far the greater proportion of their
food is vegetable matter. They eat dry material
if necessary, but prefer sweet, succulent food
such as figs, juicy pods, or seeds of acacias,

⊕ A remarkable feature of the ostrich are its enormous, gleaming eyes, complete with long lashes. Their eyes are the largest of any terrestrial vertebrate and provide excellent vision.

which are generally abundant in the less arid parts of their range. They may occasionally eat a lizard or small mouse if they can catch one, and occasionally insects such as locusts make up part of their daily diet. If a preferred source of food runs out, ostriches switch to whatever else is available, but acacias and aloes provide the staple diet almost everywhere.

Ostriches obtain all the moisture they need from the succulent plants they eat—a remarkable achievement, because they live in places that regularly reach 104° F (40° C) or more during the day. They also increase their body temperatures in hot periods, reducing the need to lose heat and thereby lose water.

Because an ostrich is so tall, it has a commanding view of the surrounding landscape. However, when it bends its neck to feed on the ground, the advantage of its high viewpoint is momentarily lost, and it can become vulnerable to predators. Therefore ostriches feed in groups, and one or two are always on the lookout while the others are feeding. They often feed close to zebras and wildebeests—extra lookouts that warn of the approach of a lion or cheetah.

Life on the Plains

Ostriches are social; across a wide African plain it is often possible to mistake a line of distant ostriches for a line of round-topped trees. There might be 100 or more in such elongated, extended flocks. Tighter groups usually consist of family gatherings, and outside the breeding season pairs or parties of five or six birds are the norm. The bigger flocks often include many immature birds but may consist largely of adult males and females. When

Remarkable Digestion

Ostriches eat many kinds of tough food. It is first gathered into a solid mass in the crop and is then swallowed—clearly visible as an uncomfortable-looking, descending bulge in the slender neck. Sand, grit, and stones are frequently swallowed to help grind the food in the gizzard. Like rheas, ostriches have a tendency to pick up bright or shiny objects and swallow them. In captivity they may even swallow wire, coins, nails, and other inedible items. The purpose is to help grind the food—much of it indigestible to other animals—in order to make the most of whatever the ostrich can eat in difficult conditions. The intestines of an ostrich are enormous, up to 46 feet (14 m) long, to help extract maximum nutrition from the food.

breeding, however, ostriches separate into pairs or groups consisting of single males accompanied by a few females.

It is fascinating to watch a group of ostriches going about their daily business. Older birds determine the timing of activities such as dust bathing and feeding simply by setting an example that the others follow. Occasionally there will be a short skirmish—one bird threatening another with open wings and raised head, its bare neck inflated, and its short, bushy tail cocked. The other bird will usually run from such a display or may lower its head and neck and point its tail downward, showing no willingness to contest the issue. Now and then, however, two birds will fight, using pecks or well-aimed kicks to settle the dispute.

Ostriches easily outrun predators such as lions if they spot them soon enough, but they may have to resort to more physical defense. A powerful kick from an ostrich can seriously maim a predator if it strikes a limb joint or can prove fatal if it strikes the head.

⊙ *A running ostrich has a huge stride, covering 11.5 feet (3.5 m) with each step. Its feet move in a high-stepping, thrusting action that gives both great speed and endurance. An ostrich may reach 43 miles per hour (69 km/h), and it can keep up a steady 30 miles per hour (48 km/h) for 30 minutes or more.*

Burying Her Head in the Sand?

When a female ostrich sits on her eggs during the day, she is at her most vulnerable—stationary, in open space, with restricted vision, and without the readiness to run that a standing ostrich enjoys. She must keep still and crouch down to avoid being seen by predators. She may even rest with her head low on the ground, probably the origin of the unlikely idea that the ostrich will bury its head in the sand. An ostrich away from the nest may also occasionally crouch as flat as it can, hoping that a nearby predator will not spot it. "Burying your head in the sand" means ignoring trouble and hoping it will go away, a fair description of this strategy. However, although the ostrich keeps its head down, it never buries it.

The dominant male is a magnificent sight as he patrols his territory and challenges subordinate males or displays to females. The display is passionate and energetic; and if the female is not ready to mate following the performance, it is repeated with equal vigor. A territorial male has another impressive part to his repertoire: a deep, roaring "boom." It is often heard late in the day or at night.

While courting his hens, the male makes a number of shallow scrapes or pits in the ground in the center of his territory, which may be from 0.8 to 5.8 square miles (2–15 sq km) in area. Having mated, he leads the female to one of the pits, and she will lay around seven eggs, one every other day over a period of two weeks. Several other hens lay in this same nest, also on alternate days. Usually, two to five other ostriches add their eggs, but sometimes as many as 18 will add eggs to the growing clutch. Only the dominant hen will stay nearby and guard the eggs against predators, which include jackals and hyenas.

Breeding Behavior

Ostriches breed in the dry season in most areas, but in some places they take advantage of the rains and breed shortly afterward, when there is a brief flush of new plant growth or an abundance of seeds. When food is scarce, as it usually is in deserts, ostriches form stable pairs. Elsewhere, when food is abundant enough to allow more ostriches to live close together, there are more complicated relationships. Usually, a mature male holds a breeding territory that includes a dominant female and several subordinate or secondary females.

The dominant male and female produce young, but the subordinate females will mate with other males and lay eggs in other nests whether they have mated with the dominant male or not. However, these eggs are not incubated and produce no chicks. Sometimes males with no territories also mate with any females they can find, but such matings do not result in the production of eggs.

⬆ During courtship the male approaches the female and waves his spread wings before throwing himself to the ground and fanning his tail. He then rolls from side to side, raising his wings and swinging his head from side to side.

⬇ Several females may lay their eggs together, but remarkably, the dominant female is able to identify her own eggs for the purposes of incubation.

The eggs are glossy white and measure about 6.25 inches (16 cm) in length. The shell is 0.08 inches (2 mm) thick and very strong. The complete clutch may number dozens of eggs, often more than 50, but only around 20 or 25 can be incubated properly by the sitting adult. The dominant female makes sure that her own eggs are in the middle of the nest and therefore most likely to hatch. Eggs laid by other hens are pushed to the edge and usually fail to hatch.

The female incubates the eggs by day, remaining well hidden as she sits low on the nest and relying on her dull, brown plumage to make her difficult to spot. The male, much more obvious in his striking black-and-white plumage, sits on the eggs during the night. After six weeks the eggs hatch. It is likely that while still inside the eggs, the chicks hear each others' calls and hatch out together.

It takes three months for the downy chicks to grow feathers, and this dull plumage lasts for two years before they molt into a more adult-like plumage. The chicks are not fully grown until around 18 months old. Young chicks are brooded by their parents or by other adults, and they are brave in their defense. They either use a display that feigns injury, luring predators away from vulnerable chicks, or they may choose to attack.

Sometimes, a family group consisting of a mother and her chicks may join with other, similar familes of ostriches. As many as 100 or more chicks of varying sizes may then be seen roaming the plains together with a small number of attendant adults.

Conservation Pressures

North African ostriches are endangered and rare. It was only recently that the Middle Eastern birds became exterminated by hunters. Ostriches and African people lived in harmony for hundreds of years, but the arrival of Europeans in Africa put immense pressure on most wildlife, ostriches included. They were hunted for meat, leather, and feathers, as well as for sport. Ostrich habitat has been damaged by overgrazing, forestry, and development, and

⊕ *Barely 10 percent of ostrich eggs hatch, and despite gathering in groups for greater safety and the care taken by the adult birds, very few chicks survive to adulthood. Those that do may live for 30 or 40 years, however.*

it faces more pressure as Africa's human population grows rapidly. In South Africa ostriches are restricted to a tiny part of their recent range, and the presence of escaped ostriches from ostrich farms may threaten the integrity of the remaining wild populations. It is only in East Africa that ostriches still thrive, and then mainly in the national parks. But even there conservation efforts must remain strong and strictly enforced.

Magical Eggs

Despite their great size and strength, the eggs of ostriches still attract the attention of predators. The eggs are sometimes broken open by jackals and hyenas. Egyptian vultures (*Neophron percnopterus*) also crack them open by repeatedly tossing stones at them until the shell breaks. Ostrich eggs are also revered in certain human cultures and have been used in traditional death rites and rituals. In some places, because they were thought to have magical properties, they have been used to protect houses from fire and lightning. The ancient Egyptians used them as symbols of justice because of their perfect symmetry. Today they are still used in art, for making jewelry, and as water containers.

Common name Emu

Scientific name *Dromaius novaehollandiae*

Family	Dromaiidae
Order	Casuariiformes

Size Height: 59–75 in (150–190 cm); weight: 66–121 lb (30–55 kg)

Key features Bulky, horizontal body with bushy brown feathers; vestigial wings and tail; heavily feathered lower neck, male has bare blue-gray upper neck; female has black upper neck and blue face; rather deep, pointed bill; long, brown legs

Habits Feeds during daylight, singly or in groups; usually seeks shade in hottest part of the day; roosts on the ground

Nesting Nest is a hollow on the ground; 5–15 eggs; incubation by the male for 56 days; chicks cared for by male and become mature at 2–3 years; 1 brood

Voice Usually silent, but some grunting and booming calls in breeding season

Diet Seeds, fruits, flowers, roots; also large insects

Habitat Open forest and semiarid plains; occasionally desert areas or suburban open spaces

Distribution Widespread in Australia

Status Stable; locally increasing

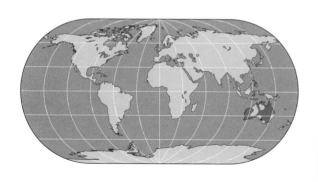

Emu

Dromaius novaehollandiae

Big, heavy bodied, and with dark, bushy plumage, the emu is the Australian counterpart of the ostrich—although it has many quite different characteristics.

EMUS ARE IMMEDIATELY IDENTIFIABLE IN THEIR Australian homeland, for they are huge and ostrichlike. Yet they are also quite different from ostriches (*Struthio camelus*) in several respects. They do not have the massive, muscular bare "thighs" of an ostrich, the body is less round, and the neck is less thin and erect. Instead, the lower neck is broad where it merges into the body but tapers upward to the small head, with a demarcation visible between the "bushy" lower neck and the slender upper part.

Males and females have mid-brown body plumage that appears fibrous, as if brushed into a coarse, layered coat hanging downward around the humpbacked body. The plumage has a "parting" along the back. The male has pale blue-gray skin on his cheeks (with a black "bristly" patch around the ear opening) and neck, with black, bristly plumage on the throat, forehead, crown, and nape. The black plumage is more extensive on the neck, nape, and forehead of the hen, and her cheeks are bluer. Both sexes have deep red eyes and dark gray bills. The legs, bearing three strong toes, are tightly feathered above the knee joint.

Plenty of Food

Emus are omnivorous, concentrating on the most easily available and most nutritious foods. Seeds, fruits, and new shoots of trees and shrubs are regularly eaten. They are usually plucked from the growing plant and swallowed with a backward jerk of the head, but some fallen fruits and seeds are picked up from the ground. Beetles, grasshoppers, and caterpillars are also frequently eaten whenever they are abundant. Emus may walk 11 to 15 miles (18–25 km) per day in search of food, although they generally seem to have little problem

⬆ Emus live in most of Australia apart from the driest interior and most developed urban areas. They are also absent from Tasmania, where a separate race of emus became extinct. Emus avoid dense forest. Grassland or light woodland make prime emu country.

 SEE ALSO Ratites **11**:16; Ostrich **11**:20; Cassowary, Southern **11**:28; Rhea, Common **11**:34; Kiwi, Brown **11**:36; Birds of Prey **15**:

finding something to eat. However, they may have difficulty finding water during dry spells. They drink regularly if water is available.

Emus spend the early part of the day eating or moving to new feeding areas. During the hottest part of the day they may find shade beneath trees and rest until it cools down. Emus lose heat by raising their wings to expose blood vessels on the underside.

Emus generally live singly or in pairs. Even when paired, they often keep 150 to 300 feet (46–90 m) apart except when drinking. However, they gather in groups when moving to new feeding areas or when concentrated at sites of preferred foods. Sometimes emus on the move to better feeding places may be brought to a temporary halt by a barrier such as a fence. When this happens, substantial numbers may build up. Even then, there is little interaction between the groups.

A strange feature of emus is their apparent curiosity regarding humans; they will watch people closely and even follow them, as long as they are not frightened by sudden noise or movement.

Caring Fathers

Mating begins by a female moving into a male's territory and attracting him with drumming calls. The male then builds a nest. Soon he is joined by the female, and after pairing, she lays her dark green eggs. The eggs are very small for such a large bird.

The pair stay together for some months, but only the male sits on the eggs. He does not feed, drink, or even produce droppings during incubation. The chicks are out of the nest and walking within a day of hatching, and the male looks after them for around five months. He will attack approaching animals at this stage, including his mate, but dingoes, foxes, and birds of prey still take some chicks.

Holding Their Own

Europeans put huge pressure on emus when colonizing Australia, and tens of thousands were killed as agricultural pests. Despite this persecution, emus remain stable and common in most areas, although numbers are reduced wherever intensive farming occurs. Emus are also highly vulnerable to dingo attacks.

⍖ *Emus within a group resolve disputes by tilting their heads down and grunting at each other. If this fails, the quarrel may involve pecking and kicking.*

Common name Southern cassowary
(double-wattled cassowary)

Scientific name *Casuarius casuarius*

Family Casuariidae

Order Casuariiformes

Size Height: 51–67 in (130–170 cm);
weight: 64–128 lb (29–58 kg)

Key features Big, black, terrestrial bird with
tiny wings and tail; shortish, slim blue neck
with red wattles; big, brown casque, or crest,
on top of head; yellow eyes; thick, pale
brown legs

Habits Solitary, shy, and elusive in deep forest; picks
food off forest floor early and late in the day,
resting during hot midday period; uses
regular paths in the forest undergrowth

Nesting Male builds a small nest on the ground; 3–5
eggs; incubation by male for 49–56 days;
young independent at 9 months; 1 brood

Voice Rumbling threat call; deep, booming notes
in display

Diet Fruit, fungi, seeds, snails, and insects picked
up from the forest floor

Habitat Thick, undisturbed rain forest; swampy areas
beside forested rivers

Distribution New Guinea, eastern Indonesia, Queensland
in Australia

Status New Guinea population stable; Australian
birds rare and decreasing

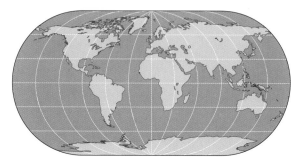

Southern Cassowary

Casuarius casuarius

*Big and powerful, but usually extremely shy, the
southern cassowary can be a fearsome adversary if
cornered, using a sharp, rapierlike claw on each foot
as a lethal weapon.*

A BLACK, FLIGHTLESS BIRD WITH almost the same
hunched, tailless shape as an emu (*Dromaius
novaehollandiae*), the cassowary is nevertheless
a dramatic-looking creature. Compared with the
emu, it is shorter-necked and slightly shorter-
legged. Like the emu, it has short, feathered,
upper legs, and it has three toes, one with a
remarkable 4-inch (10-cm) claw—a fierce
defensive weapon.

Wattles and Casque

The main features of interest on a southern
cassowary adorn its head and neck. Two
long, round, wrinkled, red wattles hang
side by side from the front of the
neck. The back of the neck is bare,
deeply wrinkled, and red. The rest of
the head and neck has bare skin of
a deep, sapphire-blue at the front,
fading to powder-blue at
the back. As with
other ratites, the
bare head allows
the large ear
openings to show clearly. The bill is relatively
long, triangular, and quite pointed. It has an
obvious downward curve and a long,
downcurved gape that gives a scowling
expression.

On top of the head a horny, flat casque, or
crest, rises from the center. Females generally
have larger casques and brighter wattles than
males. However, the size depends on the
individual, and the colors of the bare parts on
the head and neck vary with the mood of the
bird—becoming brighter during courtship or

⊕ *Cassowaries have a
flat, platelike crest called
a casque on the top of
their heads. Females
usually have larger
casques than males.*

if the bird becomes aggressive. The bright colors are probably visible in the gloom of the forest, helping cassowaries recognize each other's intentions when they meet.

The feathers of a cassowary are long, shiny, and hard, making a coarse plumage that is well able to resist the effects of daily passage through the undergrowth. The casque may also help brush aside twigs and branches, protecting the cassowary's eyes and face. The wings are tiny, and the wingtips have just five or six long, wiry, naked quills that probably help protect its body when it moves through the forest.

Forest and Woodland Dwellers

Where suitable habitat exists, cassowaries are found over most of New Guinea, except for the north and the highland areas of the interior. However, the distribution is shrinking as hunting and forest destruction take their toll. In Indonesia only one small island, Aru, supports cassowaries, and in Australia they are found in just two areas of Queensland.

Australian southern cassowaries live in dense rain forest, but they sometimes remain where forests have been partly felled if food is still available. In New Guinea they can be seen at the edge of forests, along rivers and swamps, and in more open woodland. Cassowaries seem to prefer large areas of undamaged forest; but because they are increasingly difficult to find, many are forced to live in smaller, more or less isolated patches surrounded by cleared hillsides.

A Fruit Diet

Cassowaries seem to eat fruit more than any other kind of food. Many forest plants produce fruits that fall to the ground when ripe and can then be eaten by the birds. In Australia fruits of laurels, quondongs, lilypillies, and palms form much of the diet. Ripe fruits are often knocked from the trees by feeding fruit pigeons and are eagerly devoured by a cassowary waiting below. Sometimes, succulent fruits can be found on low branches, and they are plucked direct from the tree. Cassowaries eat huge quantities of fruit, in captivity up to 6.5 pounds (3 kg) per

day. In the wild cassowaries may raid orchards and gardens if food is scarce.

Because they need fruit all year round, cassowaries must live in forests with a great variety of trees and shrubs so that fruit is always available. Forests replaced by plantations, with fruit ripening only at certain seasons, are useless for cassowaries. In Queensland southern cassowaries eat the fruits of 75 different kinds of plant, an indication of the richness and productivity of the flora in a tropical forest.

Cassowaries can be detected by the tracks they make through the forest as they feed. They wander along regular trails and cross streams at special places day after day, thus keeping the paths open even in dense jungle. The paths are also littered with large amounts of droppings, brightly colored by the fruits and seeds they eat. They are by far the best clues that cassowaries are living in an area.

Most of the cassowary's time is spent finding and eating food, with brief spells of drinking, but they rest in the heat of the day. Sometimes they seem to seek openings in the

⊕ *Cassowaries often live near rivers and are good swimmers. Here an adult and a juvenile bathe in the Australian rain forest.*

⊙ Cassowaries quickly disappear into cover if threatened. Coarse, hairlike feathers prevent damage by the foliage.

① The long central claw is a lethal weapon. The cassowary may leap up and kick with both feet at once, slashing at an intruder or a predator.

forest where they can lie quietly in the sun, provided they have instant access to deep cover should they be disturbed.

Cassowaries are more or less solitary birds except when briefly paired in the breeding season or when males are guarding the young. At such times these shy birds can become aggressive and should be treated with great

respect, especially if one is accidentally cornered. Normally, however, long before people get close enough to a cassowary to see it, the bird has heard them coming and slinks silently into the forest.

Breeding Behavior

Little is known about cassowaries in the wild. It is thought that southern cassowaries may breed at the end of the wet season, when fruits are most abundant. Males have small territories but do not seem to do much to defend them against others. Instead, they make a nest on the ground and await the arrival of a female. The female is the bigger and brighter of the two birds, but the male probably starts the courtship ritual that leads to mating. He repeatedly approaches the hen, his back feathers raised, until eventually she allows him to walk beside her. The male then puffs out the skin of his throat and makes deep, booming calls as he walks in circles around the female bird. Sometimes the roles are reversed, and it is the female that repeatedly encircles the male.

After mating, the female remains with the male for a short time and then lays her dark green eggs in the nest, which is lined with grass and leaves and well camouflaged on the forest floor. The eggs are about 5 inches (13 cm) long and weigh about 23 ounces (650 g). After laying her eggs, the female leaves to find another male with which to mate. During the breeding season she will have laid four or five clutches in separate nests with different males.

The chicks are quickly able to leave the nest and feed themselves, closely guarded by the

Successive Polyandry

Many birds are polygamous, having more than one mate, but the southern cassowary adopts a special kind of polygamous relationship. The female seeks a mate, stays with him long enough to mate and lay eggs, and then leaves him to care for the eggs and the young while she goes off in search of another male. She does this repeatedly, so that eventually the female has produced several sets of eggs all fertilized by different males.

A female ostrich may lay only seven eggs, but the male, having mated with several other females that also lay in the same nest, may hatch out 20 or so of his offspring. The female cassowary will lay up to five eggs per clutch, but as many as 25 in all, and each male has the chance to hatch out five of his young. This gives more advantage to the female. A male that has several mates is described as polygynous; a female that has several mates is polyandrous. The method used by the southern cassowary of finding several mates, one after the other, is called successive polyandry.

male. He finds fruits for them and helps them feed. From the male the chicks probably learn which types of food to eat and where to find them. The chicks remain with their father for a considerable period—usually around nine months. Birds of prey and snakes are potential predators, and the father must remain alert to guard his brood. In Queensland southern cassowaries have great difficulties rearing their young because they are so often killed by other animals that live in the forest.

The survivors may stay together for some time even after they leave the male parent.

↧ *A male southern cassowary with a chick and an unhatched egg in eastern Australia. Only the male bird incubates the eggs and looks after the young.*

Striped Chicks

Baby cassowaries, like other young ratites, are boldly patterned with neat, even, black-and-buff stripes. The youngsters keep the striped plumage for three to six months, by which time they are a quarter grown. It is then replaced by plain brown plumage. The stripes help break up the chicks' outline against a background of dead leaves and twigs in the complex light and shade of the forest floor. Baby emus have broad, neat, dark and light stripes, too, but each dark stripe has blackish edges and a rusty center. The stripes create a pattern that is equally valuable in open countryside with tall grass and dead stems. A young ostrich, however, is striped only on the head and neck and more mottled on the body.

Sacred or Simply Useful?

In some places cassowaries have been helped to survive because they are given magical or mystical significance by local tribes. One tribe in New Guinea believes the cassowary is the mother of the tribe; another that cassowaries are their female ancestors, reincarnated in the form of the great bird. These beliefs have helped preserve cassowaries from persecution.

Other tribes have no such inhibitions, however; a cassowary can feed a family for days. The feathers are also used for ceremonial decoration, as earrings, and for piercing the nose. The sharp-edged claws, such a formidable weapon for the live bird, are used to tip arrows, and the long bones are made into daggers. Cassowaries are kept in captivity in New Guinea and sold for their meat.

They have downy plumage for several months before growing brown feathers and the beginnings of the horny casque on the head. In captivity southern cassowaries may live for 40 years. In the wild it is thought that their life span is much shorter—about 12 to 19 years.

Most southern cassowaries probably remain within a small territory all their lives. In the dry season, however, they may need to move a little farther away to find a waterhole or a suitable drinking place on a river. The birds will normally only move a considerable distance from their preferred area if the forest is felled or if they are disturbed by noisy development. When this happens, cassowaries can be found very occasionally in unexpected places far from their usual habitats.

Vanishing Habitat

Like the other two cassowary species, the southern cassowary faces long-term problems as rain forest is felled at an unceasing rate. It cannot survive in small areas of forest or in plantations with too few kinds of fruit. Unbroken expanses of rich, varied forest still support healthy numbers, but such places are becoming increasingly rare. Even in Australia the rain forest is being felled at an alarming rate, and remaining tracts have big roads cut through them, which disrupts the cassowaries.

Birds are also killed by road traffic and, despite their defensive claws, attacked by dogs. Wild pigs that roam the forest also kill many chicks. In New Guinea cassowaries have been traded locally for hundreds of years. However, the hunting of cassowaries for feathers now poses a deadly threat, as western dealers fuel the illegal trade in plumes. Unlike ostriches and emus, cassowaries are difficult to breed in captivity, and the chances of creating a thriving zoo population seem small. Sadly, the future for this bird is quite bleak.

⊖ *The cassowary chicks remain with their father for about nine months, learning how to find food. It takes about two years for the chicks to develop the adult plumage and another year to become fully mature.*

Common name Common rhea (greater rhea)

Scientific name *Rhea americana*

Family	Rheidae
Order	Rheiformes

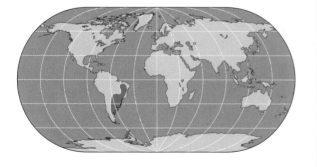

Size Height: 50–55 in (127–140 cm); weight: 44–55 lb (20–25 kg)

Key features Ostrichlike; small, round head and broad, flat bill on upright, slender, feathered neck; round body with bushy brown plumage; black chest; long, powerful, gray-brown legs

Habits Gregarious, living on bushy plains; long-striding; diurnal

Nesting Male makes nest and fights for females, which lay eggs in it as a group before leaving to mate with other males; incubation by male for 30–35 days; young mature at 2–3 years; 1 brood

Voice Deep, far-carrying, double roar or grunt; also whistling calls

Diet Mostly vegetable matter; also some insects, amphibians, reptiles, and small mammals

Habitat Grasslands such as the Brazilian campo and the Argentinian pampas

Distribution South-central Brazil southward through Uruguay, Paraguay, and Argentina

Status Declining, near-threatened

Common Rhea

Rhea americana

In South America the common rhea occupies a niche similar to the one occupied by the ostrich in Africa. In fact, the common rhea is by far the most ostrichlike of all the other ratites.

THE COMMON RHEA IS REMARKABLY like a dull-brown female ostrich (*Struthio camelus*) in general appearance. It has a similar round head and snakelike neck, a flattened bill with prominent nostrils, and big eyes. Its neck, however, is tightly feathered and lacks the color of a male ostrich. Instead, the male has an area of black plumage at the base of the neck in the breeding season. (It is brown in the hen.)

The powerful upper legs are also feathered, almost white in color, and much better developed than those of the emu (*Dromaius novaehollandiae*). Again, this is a more ostrichlike feature, for the rhea is also a high-speed runner. There are three short, thick toes on each foot. The wings are quite short but better developed than an emu's, with white underfeathers and wingtips. The long wings are extended and used to balance the bird when it dashes across the plains. The plumage is smooth and silky, but there are no tail feathers.

Greatest Range

This is the most widely distributed species of rhea, but numbers have declined recently with a consequent reduction in overall range. It can be found in Brazil east of the Amazon forests and in a wider band southward. It is also found east of the Andes to the Atlantic coast, but it does not extend so far south into Patagonia as the lesser rhea (*Pterocnemia pennata*). Various types of bushy grassland and grassy woodland are suitable for rheas. They are called pampas, campo, cerrado, and chaco depending on their characteristics—chaco being the most wooded. Very wide, open grasslands devoid of cover are

⊕ *A male rhea and his chicks grazing in typical habitat of open plains with tall grasses and scattered trees. The rhea is the largest bird found in South America.*

usually avoided by rheas. In the breeding season common rheas usually find a suitable area close to a river or lake.

Agile Feeders

Rheas are even more omnivorous than the ostrich. They eat more or less anything, animal or vegetable, that they can manage. Leaves of all kinds of plants, even spiny thistles, are a staple food, along with various seeds, fruits, and tender, juicy roots. Rheas are quick, agile, and very accurate with stabbing or grabbing movements of their head and neck, and they can often catch small rodents, frogs, and reptiles, including snakes. They also feed on abundant insects such as grasshoppers.

Rheas remain in a small area all their lives. In their habitat there is no real dry season, and there is an abundance of food. They wander around feeding for most of the day but seldom drink. If it is very hot, they may rest by day and feed by night. Rheas often mix with large mammals such as pampas deer, vicunas, or even cattle and sheep. By doing this, they help each other spot danger. Rheas can be found in groups of up to 50, except when breeding. If chased by a predator, rheas may zigzag away or suddenly squat down to avoid detection.

Complicated Mating

Males run, twist their necks together, bite, and kick in fights for females. Once a male wins the right to mate, he leads several females to a nest, and they all lay eggs there, returning every two or three days to lay more. The females then find other males with which to mate. Thus males are polygynous, and females are polyandrous at the same time. Rhea family relationships become difficult to follow!

The male may incubate as many as 30 eggs at one time, laid by perhaps a dozen females. When the eggs hatch, he looks after the chicks until they are independent. The male keeps young chicks together by whistling to them. This is especially important in long grass where visibility is very limited and in which all kinds of predators can hide in ambush.

It is not easy to look after such large numbers of young, but males fight bravely if necessary, even chasing away riders on horseback if they come too close. Sometimes families of chicks become separated, and some may join up with other groups, so that a male may be seen with chicks of several different ages together. The young stay with the male for six months and then remain with each other for another two or three years, by which time they are ready to start mating.

Illegal Trade

Sadly, common rheas are threatened by illegal hunting and the export of feathers and skins, mainly to Japan and the U.S. In 1980 as many as 50,000 birds were exported, mostly from Paraguay. Rheas are still common in parts of the chaco region, however.

Common name Brown kiwi

Scientific name *Apteryx australis*

Family	Apterygidae
Order	Apterygiformes
Size	Length: 19.5–25.5 in (50–65 cm); weight: 3–8 lb (1.4–3.6 kg)
Key features	Pear-shaped, terrestrial bird with long, thin bill and round head; no tail; stumpy legs; dense, dark brown plumage
Habits	Feeds at night; spends daytime in burrows
Nesting	Nests in burrow or cavity; up to 3 eggs; incubation 75–84 days by the male; chicks independent after 14–20 days; young males mature at 14 months, and females mature at 2 years; 1 brood
Voice	Shrill, far-carrying whistles that rise and fall in pitch; also grunts and growls
Diet	Mostly invertebrates; some seeds and leaves
Habitat	Dense rain forest; now forced to occupy scrub, thickets, and grassland edge in absence of true habitat
Distribution	Very local on both North and South Island of New Zealand and various offshore islands
Status	Declining, but not yet threatened

Brown Kiwi

Apteryx australis

Round, dumpy, and short-legged, the kiwi is famous for laying the biggest egg relative to its size of any bird in the world. It is also shy and elusive, entirely nocturnal, and difficult to observe.

THE KIWI IS A FAMILIAR image to millions of people throughout the world, even though most have never see one. It looks peculiarly rounded, having no obvious wings. It also has a hunched, round-backed body, a deep belly that envelops the tops of its short, thick legs, no tail, and a round head. It recalls a wingless, forward-leaning penguin, but with one distinctive feature—a long, slightly downcurved bill.

The kiwi's face bears several long, thin bristles, which are specially adapted feathers. The rest of the plumage resembles a shaggy coat of hair. Each feather has a soft, downy base and a stiff, waterproof tip. Most birds have a complex feather structure that uses tiny barbs and barbules to zip the vane of the feather together to form a flat blade. Kiwis, like other ratites, do not have this arrangement, and the wispy elements of the vane of the feather remain loose and free-flowing.

Unlike other ratites, the kiwi has four strong toes on each foot, each with a strong claw. The legs are quite powerful, but the forward-leaning stance and widely spread feet give an unbalanced look to a running kiwi.

The kiwi's ear openings are clearly visible, and the bird has acute hearing. It also has a good sense of smell. However, the eyes are small, and the bird's eyesight is poor.

Fragmented Range

Because of human persecution and land development the brown kiwi is the only kiwi species still found on North Island, New Zealand, and its range there is fragmented. It has also been introduced to some offshore islands as a conservation measure. On South Island it is found only in small areas on the west coast.

⊕ *A brown kiwi probes for crustaceans among the kelp on Brown Island, New Zealand.*

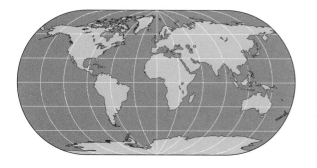

SEE ALSO Ratites **11**:16; Ostrich **11**:20; Emu **11**:26; Cassowary, Southern **11**:28; Rhea, Common **11**:34

Brown kiwis once inhabited dark, damp, rich forests and bush that flourished in the abundant temperate to subtropical climate. Practically all of this habitat has now gone, and the birds are restricted to wooded islands, bushy hillsides, plantations of exotic trees, and even farmland. Although this is a wider range of habitats, none of it is so ideally suited to the kiwi as its previous home.

Reluctant to Leave

Kiwis are nocturnal and elusive and keep to thick cover. In this respect they act like an avian version of a hedgehog. Both sexes will chase away other kiwis from their territory in the breeding season, sometimes engaging in a noisy fight to settle the issue, but they are more tolerant of intruders at other times.

Kiwis are very attached to their home ranges and may remain there even after a forest has been felled, until lack of food forces them to move. They have several burrows, which are used both as daytime refuges and when they are nesting. Unusually, the kiwi scent marks its burrows in the form of strong-smelling

Weak Eyes; Good Ears and Nose

In bright light a kiwi can see less than 3 feet (0.9 m) with its tiny eyes, although it can see about twice this distance at night. However, a kiwi can hear well and will often turn its head to listen to sounds. The ear openings are clearly visible on the side of the head and are as big, or even bigger, than the eyes. The kiwi's sense of smell is also extremely good—much more like a mammal's than a bird's. The nostrils are situated in the bulbous tip at the end of the kiwi's long bill, instead of at the base near the forehead as they are in other birds. The location of the kiwi's nostrils is a special adaptation for helping it when probing for food. A special valve at the base of the nostrils allows the kiwi to keep out mud and dirt, and it can expel unwanted items from them with a sudden snort.

Kiwis find their prey by smell, using the bill to probe into dead leaves and assorted muddy, sticky ooze under trees and bushes at night. Once prey is detected, the bill is used to snap it up or pull or dig it out. All kinds of insects, including a lot of larvae, spiders, and worms, are consumed. Fruit, seeds, and leaves are also frequently eaten but make up only a small proportion of the diet.

droppings—one of several aspects of kiwi lifestyles and biology that have similarities with the mammals rather than the birds.

Paired for Life

Unlike the other members of the ratites, the brown kiwi has a simple breeding arrangement; pairs stay together for life, away from other pairs, and nest in a burrow. The hen lays up to three eggs that measure around 4.5 to 5.5 inches (11.5–14 cm) in length and weigh 15 ounces (425 g). They are proportionately the biggest eggs in the world of birds. Not surprisingly, the female kiwi lays her eggs 25 to 30 days apart. If the clutch is eaten by a predator, the female will lay again, sometimes two or three times.

The incubation period is long at about 80 days, and the male incubates the eggs alone. He may not begin incubation for up to two weeks after the female has left the burrow, and he may not settle down to the task with any real concentration for another 20 or 30 days. The male leaves the burrow to feed each night, often for four or five hours at a time and sometimes for much longer. Thus the eggs are left uncovered for an exceptionally long period

of time. The body temperature of the male kiwi is only 100.4° F (38° C), which is unusually low for a bird. The long, drawn-out incubation procedure, carried out at a surprisingly low temperature, is yet another of the kiwi's more extraordinary attributes.

The chicks hatch out over a long period, too; there may up to 15 days between them. They have no egg tooth (the small, bony point on the bill tip that enables most birds to break out from their egg), and they must force the shell apart with their feet and bills. Once hatched, the chicks look just like miniature adults. Even when only five or six days old, they are able to move off to feed on their own, but

⊕ *A brown kiwi preens itself at the entrance to the nest burrow. The burrow may be up to 6.5 feet (2 m) deep. While the male incubates the eggs, the female stays in another burrow close by.*

now the unofficial national symbol of New Zealand, was given absolute protection in 1921. But since then numbers have still plummeted. Hunting for food and feathers continues, illegally, but other pressures have also contributed. The forest habitat of the kiwi has been felled with little concern for the future, and in the few places it remains, native rain forest is still being cleared to make way for plantations or to build houses.

Humans took rabbits to New Zealand, and they quickly became a menace to crops. So stoats and weasels were introduced to kill the rabbits. These predators wreak havoc among New Zealand's birds, not least the kiwis. Cats and dogs were also introduced, and, if anything, proved even more destructive; a single dog is credited with killing 500 kiwis out of 900 on one island in just two months. People also began to lay traps for possums, and the traps inevitably caught hundreds of kiwis as well. The story of western development and the kiwi has not been a happy one.

Fortunately, conservation measures are being taken, and introductions to islands such as Little Barrier Island, Kapiti Island, Hen Island, and D'Urbille Island have helped put kiwis in places where they should be safe.

they are brooded by day in the burrow by the male, and the female now makes regular visits to the nest-burrow.

The chicks are fully independent in the remarkably short time of 14 to 20 days, but they may remain with their parents for a while longer. Rarely, brown kiwi chicks may remain with their parents for a year or more after hatching. The chicks are not fully grown until they are 18 months old, and until then they are vulnerable to many predators.

History of Persecution

Kiwis have always been hunted for meat and feathers, and the Maori people, arrivals from Polynesia, wiped them out from several places. Nevertheless, the kiwi had a symbolic significance for the Maori, who believed it was specially protected by Tane, the god of the forest. It did not, however, reduce the predeliction for hunting kiwis, but merely ensured more careful, ritual preparation for kiwi hunts. The first kiwi killed on a hunt was offered to Tane to appease him.

Once European settlers arrived, kiwis were hunted even more effectively. However, it was not until hunting for food was replaced by hunting for trade in feathers (they were sent to Europe to make "fur" muffs and other fashion items) that kiwis became really endangered. They were slaughtered in large numbers, and their range on the mainland much reduced.

Hunting was banned in 1908, and the kiwi,

⊕ *A kiwi egg is proportionately huge—up to one-fifth of the female's body weight. The yolk occupies 60 percent of the egg's volume.*

Territorial Marking

An activity that is extremely rare in birds, but very common in mammals, is that of marking territory with strong-smelling droppings. Kiwis mark territorial boundaries and occupied burrows in this way. Although a kiwi can cover long distances on nightly forages—as much as 2 miles (3.2 km)—it remains in its territory for life, provided there is always food available. Even when the habitat has been damaged or destroyed, a kiwi will remain in the territory if it can. A kiwi usually has several burrows scattered around its territory, and they are used as daytime shelters or resting places at night. Some burrows may be used night after night by one or both birds. Others may only be used occasionally by the birds over a long period. All of the burrows will be marked by fresh scent whenever the territorial kiwi passes by.

The Tinamou Family Tinamidae

Small, round-bodied, short-billed, and short-legged, tinamous resemble partridges or francolins. They are also similar in appearance to the bustards. Tinamous are placed in their own order, the Tinamiformes. They form an ancient group of birds, with a fossil record stretching back for 10 million years.

In the scheme of the world's bird families tinamous fit close to the original "ratite ancestor" before that bird evolved into the groups we now see, such as the rheas, ostriches, and emus. The tinamous probably separated from the ancestral stock before the ratites became modified by isolation, and they have kept fully functional wings and a deep keel on the breastbone—both crucial to powered flight. Despite this fundamental difference, the tinamous and ratites seem in every other respect to be closer to each other than to any other bird groups.

The New World tinamous and Old World partridges are a good example of convergent, or parallel, evolution. The two groups are not closely related but have similar lifestyles, foods, and habitats and have developed along very similar lines. In a way, it can be seen as evolution doing the same thing, quite separately, in different parts of the world. Early European travelers to South America thought tinamous were partridges and called them "perdiz," which is Spanish for partridge.

Ungainly Landings
Tinamous are generally small birds, although the largest are about the size of a domestic chicken. Several species have crests that can be raised in alarm and excitement. They have little or no tail; longer tail coverts often cover

the true tail feathers; and the birds look blunt and rounded, with wide, densely feathered backs. The wings are small, round, and rather weak, but flight can be sustained for a short distance with quick, fairly powerful wingbeats. Tinamous fly with a special "sideslipping" action that is ideal for avoiding aerial predators.

Without a tail, however, flying tinamous often experience difficulties in flight. They have no "airbrake" other than their wings, and they must therefore land at full speed. The lack of a tail means they cannot steer easily, and they sometimes dash headlong into wires, fences, posts, and even buildings. The vanes of the feathers, normally linked together by tiny hooks and barbs, are fused solidly together in tinamous. In flight the feathers make an unusual, loud whistling noise.

The legs are strong and partridgelike, with three forward-facing toes; some species have a fourth, backward-facing toe set high on the leg. Tinamous walk with a curious delicacy and precision. They step very quietly and with great care, sometimes pausing partway through a stride but always perfectly balanced. If disturbed, they prefer to run than to fly.

Exploiting Many Habitats
Tinamous are found almost throughout South America and through Central America to northern Mexico. They have managed to find a place in almost all the habitats on the continent, from forest to open land, from sea level to mountainsides, and from the tropics to the cold south.

Although they are found in such a wide variety of habitats, tinamous all live in more or less the same way—walking on the ground and feeding on shoots, buds, seeds, and small invertebrates. They are unable to take food from high up in the vegetation, so they exploit whatever opportunities they can on the ground. Each type of tinamou is specially adapted to its habitat, and that leaves them vulnerable should that habitat be lost or threatened by human development and destruction.

Family Tinamidae: 9 genera, 47 species, including:

Crypturellus	21 species, including little tinamou (*C. soui*); undulated tinamou (*C. undulatus*); Magdalena tinamou (*C. saltuarius*)
Nothoprocta	7 species, including Andean tinamou (*N. pentlandii*); ornate tinamou (*N. ornata*); highland tinamou (*N. bonapartei*)
Tinamus	5 species, including great tinamou (*T. major*)
Eudromia	2 species, including elegant crested tinamou (*E. elegans*)

⊛ *An undulated tinamou. This species is found in scrub and forest in the northern part of South America. Inset: the highland tinamou of the Costa Rican cloud forest lays glossy green eggs in a scrape on the ground.*

Elegant Crested Tinamou

Eudromia elegans

A rather large, striking tinamou found in the southern parts of South America, this bird is shy and elusive, tending to stand stockstill or crouch close to the ground if danger threatens.

Common name Elegant crested tinamou

Scientific name *Eudromia elegans*

Family Tinamidae

Order Tinamiformes

Size Length: 14.5–16 in (37–41 cm); wingspan: 32–35 in (81–89 cm); weight: 1.4 lb (0.6 kg)

Key features Dark brown or pale, yellow-brown bird with a double white stripe on side of face; paler belly; upswept, wispy crest on head; very short-tailed and short-legged; legs bluish or whitish (depending on subspecies) with no hind toes

Habits Found in groups; wanders widely in search of food

Nesting Nest is a scrape on the ground; 5–6 eggs; incubation 20–21 days; young fledge after 7 days; 1, sometimes 2, broods

Voice Flutelike, whistling call

Diet Omnivorous, taking a wide variety of invertebrates, seeds, and fruit

Habitat Dry to arid grassland and bushy savanna

Distribution Southern Chile and Argentina

Status Locally common but generally declining

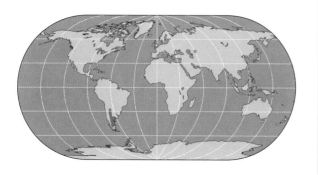

THE ELEGANT CRESTED TINAMOU IS A SMALL-HEADED, round-bodied bird. Ten subspecies are recognized, each with markedly different plumage and differing substantially in size. The subspecies *multiguttata* of eastern Argentina is at the dark end of the range; its plumage is mid-gray-brown with copious bars and long black streaks. The palest subspecies, *albida,* is found in the west of Argentina; it has much yellower plumage. All subspecies have paler plumage on the belly than elsewhere, with rounded pale spots on the upper parts.

The most striking patterning in all subspecies is seen on the head; there is a curved pale stripe behind the eye, a longer white streak from the bill across the cheek, and a pale throat patch. The crest feathers are up to 3 inches (7.5 cm) long, pointed, and stand erect or swept backward. The small, dark gray bill is downcurved and pointed. This is the only species of tinamou that lacks a hind toe.

Mainly Lowland

The elegant crested tinamou occurs in a narrow strip of land straddling the Argentina-Chile border as well as in a broader area that stretches across to the east coast of southern Argentina, south to Santa Cruz. Although mostly a lowland species, it does locally reach 8,200 feet (2,500 m) or more in the Andean foothills. In summer insect food is abundant, and the bird then eats all kinds of invertebrate prey, but at other times it is mainly a seed-eater. Seeds of several species of grasses are taken, as well as leaves, buds, and fruit, depending on what is available.

 SEE ALSO Tinamou Family, The **11**:40; Game Birds **11**:44; Birds of Prey **15**:8

In the main it is a sedentary bird, especially during the breeding season when food is plentiful. At other times, however, the elegant crested tinamou may be forced to undertake quite long-distance movements in search of food supplies. At such times small family groups may join together in larger bands of as many as 50 to 100 birds, sometimes moving into irrigated areas. The elegant crested tinamou is strictly terrestrial. It will regularly roost in scrapes beside bushes, which then become copiously marked with droppings as a result.

Male Incubators

Most individuals nest in October, making a simple nest of grasses and twigs in the shelter of a small bush. The eggs have a glossy, almost polished appearance when laid. The males are highly territorial during breeding, calling noisily and being answered by neighboring birds. Males may fight other intruding males in quite fierce encounters, using their feet and wings. Females sometimes chase intruding females, too, but usually a male attracts two or more hens by his calls and mates with them.

After laying their eggs, the hens may later move on to mate with another male. After they have mated again, females sometimes mate with yet more males, each time leaving the males to incubate the eggs and care for the young. This pattern in breeding allows for efficient and rapid reproduction.

Slow Decline in Numbers

This is not a rare or threatened bird, but it has shown a long-term decline and could become vulnerable in the future. The reduction in its range began during the twentieth century. The decline appears to be due to hunting pressure, especially in the western mountains where this activity is intense. Skunks, foxes, wildcats, and birds of prey take adults and chicks but have little effect on healthy populations.

The species has been bred in captivity for 100 years, and large numbers were taken to Germany in an unsuccessful attempt to establish it as a game bird.

⊕ The elegant crested tinamou is found in dry, open woodland, savanna, and also in the Andean steppes on bare hillsides with scattered patches of bushes and cultivation or sandy areas with thornbush and evergreen shrubs. In Patagonia it prefers to occupy valleys down to sea level.

Game Birds

Phasianidae, Cracidae, Tetraonidae, Megapodiidae, Numididae, Meleagrididae

The many and varied game birds are grouped within the order Galliformes. Game birds share a number of features reminiscent of domestic fowl; indeed, one species of game bird, the red jungle fowl, is the ancestor of the familiar farmyard chicken. Game birds feed mainly on the ground by scratching around for seeds and other food items with their strong feet and claws, although some species of grouse feed in trees at certain times of the year. Like chickens, game birds peck food from the ground with quick, stabbing movements.

Game birds have short, broad, stiff wings whose feathers are often fingered (held open) at the tip when fully spread. They tend to fly only for short distances, with little maneuverability, but typically at considerable speed. Game birds are "sprinters" in the bird world—very quick flyers over short distances, but soon exhausted. The

Family Phasianidae: 48 genera, 183 species, including:

Francolinus	42 species, including crested francolin (*F. sephaena*)
Lophura	12 species, including silver pheasant (*L. nycthemera*)
Coturnix	9 species, including common quail (*C. coturnix*)
Alectoris	7 species, including red-legged partridge (*A. rufa*)
Tragopan	5 species, including satyr tragopan (*T. satyra*)
Gallus	4 species, including red jungle fowl (*G. gallus*)
Crossoptilon	4 species, including blue eared-pheasant (*C. auritum*)
Callipepla	4 species, including Gambel's quail (*C. gambelii*)
Colinus	3 species, including northern bobwhite (*C. virginianus*)
Perdix	3 species, including gray partridge (*P. perdix*)
Cyrtonyx	2 species, including Montezuma quail (*C. montezumae*)
Pavo	2 species, including Indian peafowl (*P. cristatus*)
Chrysolophus	2 species, golden pheasant (*C. pictus*); Lady Amherst's pheasant (*C. amherstiae*)
Phasianus	2 species, including common pheasant (*P. colchicus*)
Argusianus	1 species, great argus (*A. argus*)
Ithaginis	1 species, blood pheasant (*I. cruentus*)
Rheinardia	1 species, crested argus (*R. ocellata*)

Family Cracidae: 11 genera, 50 species, including:

Penelope	15 species, including crested guan (*P. purpurascens*); Andean guan (*P. montagnii*); white-crested guan (*P. pileata*)
Crax	12 species, including great curassow (*C. rubra*)
Ortalis	12 species, including plain chachalaca (*O. vetula*)
Aburria	4 species, including common piping guan (*A. pipile*)
Mitu	4 species, including crestless curassow (*M. tomentosa*); razor-billed curassow (*M. tuberosa*)

Family Tetraonidae: 7 genera, 16 species, including:

Tetrao	4 species, including capercaillie (*T. urogallus*); black grouse (*T. tetrix*)
Tympanuchus	3 species, including prairie chicken (*T. cupido*)
Lagopus	3 species, including willow grouse (*L. lagopus*)
Centrocercus	1 species, sage grouse (*C. urophasianus*)

Family Megapodiidae: 6 genera, 19 species, including:

Megapodius	11 species, including dusky scrub fowl (*M. freycinet*)
Leipoa	1 species, mallee fowl (*L. ocellata*)
Alectura	1 species, Australian brush turkey (*A. lathami*)

Family Numididae: 4 genera, 6 species

Guttera	2 species, including crested guinea fowl (*G. pucherani*)
Agelastes	2 species, including black guinea fowl (*A. niger*)
Numida	1 species, helmeted guinea fowl (*N. meleagris*)
Acryllium	1 species, vulturine guinea fowl (*A. vulturinum*)

Family Meleagrididae: 2 genera, 2 species

Meleagris	1 species, common turkey (*M. gallopavo*)
Agriocharis	1 species, ocellated turkey (*A. ocellata*)

↪ *With tail feathers fanned and throat feathers extended, a male capercaillie proclaims his territory and calls for a mate. A turkeylike bird, the capercaillie is the largest member of the grouse family (Tetraonidae).*

 SEE ALSO Bobwhite, Northern **11:**50; Peafowl, Indian **11:**52; Pheasant, Common **11:**56; Jungle Fowl, Red **11:**60; Partridge, Gray: 1

power for fast flight comes from large pectoral muscles anchored against a deep breastbone. This feature gives many game birds a round-bodied, deep-chested shape and allows for fast, deep wingbeats. Game birds usually fly with short, rapid wingbeats, followed by long glides.

Pheasants and Quails

The family Phasianidae includes the pheasants, quails, and partridges. The males of many pheasant species have gaudy plumage with intricate feather patterns and long, arched tails. Some have highly colored bare facial skin,

wattles, or crests and fanlike ruffs of broad, overlapping feathers. Females are usually smaller but still beautifully marked with bars and spots in a rich variety of camouflage patterns. The eared-pheasants (genus *Crossoptilon*) of China and Tibet are the only ones in which male and female look alike.

The argus pheasants (genera *Rheinardia* and *Argusianus*) and the Indian peafowl have the most glorious ornamentation of all. The "tail" of the peacock is in fact formed by the tail coverts—the greatly elongated, patterned feathers that lie over the true tail.

↑ *Although classified as ground birds, many species of game birds—like this male golden pheasant—will often take to the trees for shelter and sometimes even to find food.*

Remarkable Diversity

Most species of game birds are fairly distinct and easily recognizable. However, there may be a long list of races, or subspecies, within a species, usually characterized by variations in plumage. Such variations can often make identification difficult. In the northern bobwhite, for example, no fewer than 22 races are recognized. The widespread race *virginianus* has a black crown, a black band across the cheeks, a long, white band over the eye, and a white throat. However, in some races the white is restricted, dull, or absent. The black-headed races often lack the typical white spotting on the underparts of those found in the U.S., but there are all kinds of colorful combinations.

The common, or ring-necked, pheasant has 31 races (34 if the green pheasant is included, although it is often regarded as a separate species). Some are "ring-necked," with a white collar, but many are not. One group of races has largely white wings; some have chestnut rumps; others have green or orange rumps. Other pheasants, such as the golden pheasant, have no racial variations.

↑ *A male Montezuma quail in Arizona. It is a bird of mountainous, arid country that can withstand long periods without water.*

They are fanned into a magnificent display in front of the female. The common pheasant has been introduced as a game bird for shooting in many parts of the world. Other pheasants, such as Lady Amherst's pheasant, have also been introduced as ornamental birds. These new populations may play an important conservation role in the future as the birds' natural habitats are lost.

Blood pheasants are fairly small and rounded; they have several sharp, backward-pointing spurs on their legs. The tragopans (genus *Tragopan*) of the Himalayas and other mountain ranges in Asia have short tails, but the males still have beautifully marked plumage.

The New World quails are small, round, dapper birds with a variety of bold head patterns or tall, erect, feathery crests. Many have rich rufous plumage colors and barred or spotted patterns. They have stronger bills and longer legs than Old World quails and are more upright when

SEE ALSO Grouse, Willow **11:66**; Grouse, Sage **11:70**; Chicken, Prairie **11:74**; Turkey, Common **11:76**; Mallee Fowl **11:82**

Winter Mortality

Partridges usually remain in a small area all year, feeding on food items on the ground. However, when heavy snowfalls occur, their food is impossible to reach. When this happens, partridges move to where they can find something to eat and then return to their home territories as soon the weather improves. In the fall the size of the average flock, or covey, is 10 to 15, but by the end of the winter it is down to 5 or 7 due partly to winter mortality and also the departure of paired birds for their breeding territories. As with most other game birds, the large clutch size is an adaptation to the heavy mortality of chicks in summer and young birds in the winter, allowing at least a few chicks to live long enough to breed and replenish the species.

moving around. They live in a large area from Canada south to southern Brazil, in a variety of habitats from deep forest, open plains, and rocky mountain slopes. The northern bobwhite has a striped head pattern but no crest. Gambel's quail is typical of the crested types.

The Old World quails include the common quail of Europe, which migrates south each fall into Africa but has been reduced by intensive farming combined with large-scale trapping along the North African coast. In spring it is difficult to see in growing crops, but it is easy to hear the male's trisyllabic calls.

The partridges are smaller and more dumpy than New World quails, but still larger and stronger-billed than the Old World quails. The gray partridge of Europe is typical of farmland with meadows and hedgerows, but intensive farming has caused a widespread decline, especially through a reduction in the numbers of insects available to the young chicks. The red-legged partridge is more boldly patterned, with a pale face outlined with black, and black, rufous, and white bars on the flanks.

Francolins are a fairly uniform African and Asian group, although there is much variation in color and patterning, and there are different combinations of leg and bill colors. They are noisy birds, and the African bush and forest often ring to the calls of francolins and guinea fowl at dawn and dusk.

⊕ The vulturine guinea fowl is a tall, long-legged, and upright species with vivid red eyes, long, pointed neck plumes, and areas of intense blue and chestnut plumage. It lives in semiarid thornbush in Africa. Flocks sometimes follow monkeys to scavenge on fallen fruit.

⬆ *A group of adult helmeted guinea fowl join forces to chase away a snake that is threatening their chicks.*

Guans, Curassows, and Chachalacas

The family Cracidae consists of small-headed birds with short, strong, curved bills and fairly large, bulky bodies. Some species, such as the great curassow, have long legs. The larger species also have full, broad tails, but small ones are very short-tailed. The Cracidae are found in the extreme southern U.S. and Central and South America, and they more or less occupy the same niches as those taken by the pheasants in Asia.

All species of guans have dark plumage with long, black tails and bare red skin on the face and throat. The 14 species of curassows are round-bodied, long-tailed birds. Some have short, feathery head crests, and others have upright "helmets" on their foreheads. The chachalacas are gray-brown, long-tailed birds with broad wings. Chachalacas look somewhat pheasantlike.

⬇ *The rare ocellated turkey is much smaller than the common turkey and lacks the brushlike bristles on its chest. The bird gets its common name because of the eye spots on its tail.*

Grouse

The members of the grouse family, or Tetraonidae, are widespread in the Northern Hemisphere in Asia, Europe, and North America where they inhabit forests, prairies, and tundra. Many members of the family have intricate, beautiful, cryptic plumage patterns that allow them to blend with their surroundings. Several species have complex courtship riutuals, with males performing mock fights at special display grounds called leks. Some species turn white in winter to help them hide in snow.

Scrub Fowl, Mallee Fowl, and Brush Turkeys

The family Megapodiidae, also known as megapodes, are mostly fairly large, turkeylike birds, although a number of the smaller species are more partridgelike and have small, pointed crests and bare skin on their faces. The brush turkeys are blackish with distinctive tails that are ridged in the center and folded down the middle. Megapodes are found in New Guinea and Australia, generally in dense, tropical rain-forest habitats. The mallee fowl, however, is a species that lives in the semiarid scrublands of Australia.

The remarkable feature that distinguishes the megapodes is their nesting behavior. Instead of laying eggs in a nest and then sitting on them while the chicks grow inside, megapodes lay their eggs in a hole in the ground or in a specially built mound. In some species eggs are simply laid in sandy soil, covered over, and incubated by heat from the soil and sunshine. The more complex methods involve building a mound of loose, sandy soil over the top of a shallow pit filled with rotting vegetation. The eggs are laid in a central chamber above the rotting material and protected by the soil. The vegetable material creates heat as it rots.

The mounds of the dusky scrub fowl may be 39 feet (12 m) across and 13 feet (4 m) high. Several pairs of birds build each mound. Brush turkeys build smaller mounds with a great deal of moist, warm plant material, creating more than enough heat as it rots. The birds test the temperature of the mound by probing it with their bills. When the temperature is just right, the female lays her eggs, and the male then takes over the duties of looking after them.

Guinea Fowl

Members of the family Numididae are found in Africa and on nearby islands, although in many parts of the world some types are kept as farmyard animals. Guinea fowl are basically gray birds, but most are marked with copious white spots arranged in a beautiful, regular, and intricate pattern. Some species also have "helmets" in the form of horny crests. The crested guinea fowl, a forest species, has a tuft of upright feathers in a curious topknot. The black guinea fowl, the smallest member of the family, lacks the typical white spots. It lives in undisturbed forest and is extremely shy and hard to see. In contrast, the helmeted guinea fowl lives on open savannas and in open woodland and is a noisy, familiar, and easily observed bird of African game parks. Like many other game birds, guinea fowl have strong legs and feet with tough, arched claws, which are ideal for a life spent walking or running on the ground.

Turkeys

The family Meleagrididae consists of just two species. The common turkey of the U.S. and Mexico is the wild ancestor of the domestic turkey. The ocellated turkey has a much smaller range in Mexico, Belize, and Guatemala.

Courtship Displays

The essential aim in life for any bird is to reproduce—to rear young that will help continue the species. The hen tries to choose the "best" mate—the one most likely to produce the strongest, fittest young that are most likely to survive to breed themselves. Males may also seek the "best" mate, or they may simply try to mate with as many hens as possible, to give the best possible chance of success. In some species these roles are reversed.

Within a species a bird generally maintains a distance between itself and others. It may require a large area for itself to provide sufficient food. Even when they live in flocks, birds still maintain their distance. But contact, obviously, is essential for breeding to be successful. Pair-bonding is also vital for many species if the young are to be reared successfully. To break down barriers that would otherwise prevent physical contact and bonding, birds use a variety of courtship displays. They attract birds of the opposite sex and repel or deter those of the same sex. They also remove, if only temporarily, the overriding reluctance to allow another bird to get close.

Courtship displays are highly ritualized and specific. They must trigger the correct response inherited by the other individual. A peacock, fanning his train of eyed feathers, would not impress a peahen unless she was "programmed" to respond to the size of the train and number of eye spots within it. Every male peacock has eyed feathers, but the male that wins the female has the most eyes and the biggest train. Courtship behavior may have a secondary function. Male birds as varied as robins (*Erithacus rubecula*) and common terns (*Sterna hirundo*), for example, feed their mates during courtship. This encourages bonding and gives the hen extra nutrition when she is producing an energy-packed clutch of eggs. Pair-bonding may continue throughout the breeding season.

⬅ *Male black grouse displaying at their lek.*

➡ *A male golden pheasant using his neck cape for display.*

Northern Bobwhite

Colinus virginianus

Calling loudly from low, dense cover, the northern bobwhite is a common species in North America. It will keep out of sight until almost stepped on, when it bursts into the air with a tremendous clatter of wings.

Common name Northern bobwhite (bobwhite)

Scientific name *Colinus virginianus*

Family Phasianidae

Order Galliformes

Size Length: 8–10 in (20–25 cm); wingspan: 17 in (43 cm); weight: 4 oz (113 g)

Key features Small, rounded, rusty-brown quail with tiny bill; males have very variable head pattern—according to race—from all-black to blackish, with buff or white stripe over eye and on throat; both sexes unmarked or spotted white below; females generally duller

Habits Ground-dwelling; found in small family parties

Nesting Shallow nest on ground; 10–15 eggs; incubation 23 days; young fledge after 14 days; 1 brood

Voice Clear, whistled "bob-white!" and "kal-oi-kee?"

Diet Seeds and fruits; insects in summer

Habitat Open woodland, woodland edge and shrubbery, arable fields, pastures, and open grassland

Distribution Eastern U.S. south into Central America; also Cuba

Status Abundant; more than 20 million shot annually in U.S.

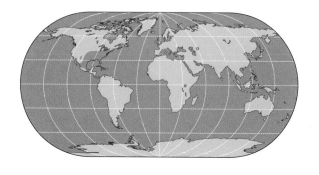

THE NORTHERN BOBWHITE IS AN UNUSUALLY variable New World quail, with 22 races and even some variation within them. All are small, round birds with no obvious crest and a stubby, black bill. Males have fairly distinct head patterns, with a buff or white stripe over the eye and on the throat, separated by broad bands of black. Some races have all-black heads and deep rufous bodies, while those with strong head patterns tend to have paler colors with a scattering of big, pale spots.

Range and Habitat

The northern bobwhite is found as far north as the Great Lakes and west to central Texas but is mostly absent from the western U.S. In the south it extends through Mexico to Guatemala, and it is also found widely in Cuba, where it is assumed to be native but could perhaps have been introduced long ago. It has certainly been introduced, with varying success, in many parts of the world, including Hawaii and New Zealand. Introductions in Britain failed to produce any lasting presence there, however.

Within its range the bird usually occupies more or less open ground, but in some areas it lives in extensive pine woods. Fields with hedges and patches of bushes or shrubbery are also favored, especially those of arable crops that provide seed and fruit.

Calling its Name

Northern bobwhites live in coveys (groups), consisting of several families together. They are terrestrial birds, keeping to thick cover mostly, but their loud calls betray their presence even if

SEE ALSO Game Birds **11**:44; Pheasant, Common **11**:56; Jungle Fowl, Red **11**:60; Partridge, Gray **11**:64

⇩ *A male bobwhite (left) is distinguished by his white eye stripe and white throat markings. Females (right) have duller plumage.*

they are hard to see. From these hidden coveys comes a chorus of questioning, triple-note calls with loud, two-note responses. The usual call gives the bird its name—a clearly pronounced "bob-white!" If approached too closely, northern bobwhites simply crouch quietly out of sight or scuttle away through the vegetation. Only if almost stepped on will they suddenly fly, bursting up underfoot in all directions. They spend all day feeding, dusting, or sunbathing and roost on the ground at night.

In natural habitats with plenty of coarse, herbaceous growth bobwhites eat the seeds of plants as varied as thistles, grasses, and oak trees (acorns are eaten with relish). Crops such as sunflowers, corn, soya, and tomatoes are also eaten. In summer this vegetarian diet is supplemented by insects. Insects are important to growing chicks and also to females that need a higher energy intake in order to produce a large clutch of eggs.

Large Broods

Northern bobwhites are monogamous. Each male displays to a female and pairs with her before making a simple, shallow nest on the ground with a lining of grasses and stems. The nest is well hidden in vegetation. After the eggs are laid, a second female will sometimes lay in the nest in a form of brood parasitism. By laying her eggs in other nests, she is giving her own eggs a better chance of success.

The chicks leave the nest soon after hatching, tended by the parent birds or by the female alone, and they grow quickly. As with many game-bird chicks, the wing feathers of bobwhite chicks grow especially quickly, and the birds are able to fly before they are fully grown, when just two weeks old.

Like other New World quails, northern bobwhites lay large numbers of eggs because many chicks die before they reach adulthood. Also, if a clutch is lost—for example, through predation—the birds will lay a replacement. These activities are designed to ensure the birds' populations are maintained at high levels.

Losses and Gains

Northern bobwhites have long been declining in traditional habitats in the south and west of their range because of land development and loss of habitat. However, in the east they have increased due to management of their numbers and habitats—despite the birds being shot for sport in huge numbers every year.

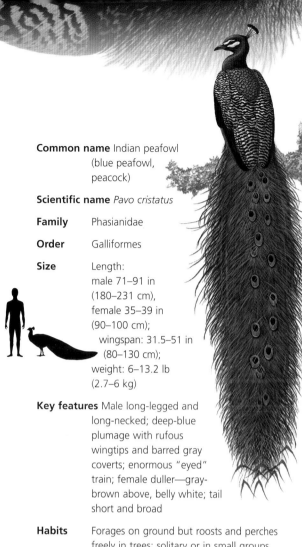

Indian Peafowl

Pavo cristatus

Common name Indian peafowl (blue peafowl, peacock)

Scientific name *Pavo cristatus*

Family Phasianidae

Order Galliformes

Size Length: male 71–91 in (180–231 cm), female 35–39 in (90–100 cm); wingspan: 31.5–51 in (80–130 cm); weight: 6–13.2 lb (2.7–6 kg)

Key features Male long-legged and long-necked; deep-blue plumage with rufous wingtips and barred gray coverts; enormous "eyed" train; female duller—gray-brown above, belly white; tail short and broad

Habits Forages on ground but roosts and perches freely in trees; solitary or in small groups

Nesting Nests on or near ground; 3–6 eggs; incubation by female for 28–30 days; young fledge after 21–28 days; 1 brood

Voice Loud, nasal clanging or trumpeting sound and short, braying sound from male; also "kok-kok" alarm call

Diet Seeds, grain, buds, and berries; also insects, small reptiles, and rodents

Habitat Open forest, orchards, and cultivation

Distribution Throughout India, parts of Pakistan, and Sri Lanka

Status Secure but locally scarce; in some areas still common and thriving

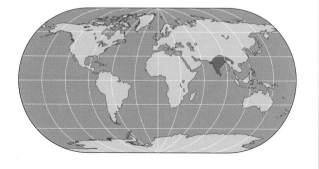

Few birds have acquired the international recognition of the male Indian peafowl or peacock, whose fanned array of "eyed" feathers has become a famous symbol of proud, showy extravagance in many countries.

A MALE PEAFOWL'S MOST OBVIOUS feature is his magnificent train, but in fact he has beautiful plumage all over. He has an upright tuft of feathers on the crown, rufous wings, and an intensely blue head, neck, and upper body—they all add greatly to his appearance. The "peacock blue" of the neck, in particular, is one of the most attractive colors seen in the game birds, gleaming even in the depths of a thick forest.

The tail feathers are relatively short and stiff and support the train of greatly elongated upper tail coverts that form the "tail." These remarkable feathers grow longer each year as the bird matures. After two years they develop magnificent "eyes," each with a central blue spot surrounded by orange, green, and cream ovals. Each feather has a stiff, spiky tip with long, wispy barbs. The feathers of the back and rump are iridescent green with orange-brown centers, each fringed with a blue-black line.

By contrast, the female is almost entirely lacking bright colors, other than some blue-green on the head and neck. She has a similar crest, but is blackish and white on the neck and chest, gray-brown above, and white beneath. Both sexes have stout, arched, short bills and long, strong legs with thick, bare shanks. Young birds are very like the female.

Locally Common

The Indian subcontinent forms a neat, triangular patch on the map that is occupied by Indian peafowl. They live in Pakistan, east of the Indus River, and may still be found in Bangladesh, although it is possible that they are extinct

 SEE ALSO Game Birds **11**:44; Pheasant, Common **11**:56

there, despite once being common. In Sri Lanka peafowl remain common in many parts, at least in the larger wooded national parks.

In India the peafowl is a sacred bird, well protected and free from persecution. Because of this it sometimes adopts a semidomesticated lifestyle around villages, temples, and other buildings. Its natural habitat, however, is stands of relatively open, mixed forest with thickets beside streams and old, tall trees in which it can

roost. The peafowl is now also found in many orchards and in cultivated areas, usually close to a stream. Peacocks can be found up to 5,900 feet (1,800 m)—sometimes even higher—in the foothills of the Himalayas.

Elegant Walkers

This is a social bird, but for much of the year adult males and females live separately, with young birds of both sexes staying with the

⊕ *The dramatic display of the male Indian peafowl is a common sight in many ornamental parks and gardens, where these birds are often kept.*

Calling from the Trees

A peafowl is a large bird; but when sitting within the canopy of a big tree, even the spectacular male can be remarkably difficult to see. He is, however, easy to hear at dusk and dawn, when the forest echoes to the sound of peacocks calling from the trees. Their calls are less beautiful than their appearance, unfortunately—in fact, they make a dreadful noise. Peacocks sometimes call at night, too. And just like common pheasants (*Phasianus colchicus*), they are likely to call loudly, all at once, after a sudden noise such as a thunderclap. They also warn all the forest inhabitants when a big cat such as a leopard is on the prowl. Females and males both make a short, hard "kok-kok" alarm call, while males also have a call that sounds rather like a braying donkey, as well as their loud, nasal, trumpeting call.

and superb eyesight and hearing, and they make the most of these senses at all times.

After drinking, peafowl usually move off into the forest to spend the hottest part of the day in the shade. They spend much time preening and dust bathing to keep their feathers in peak condition. Each evening they emerge again into more open places to feed and drink, before returning to the forest to roost, safe from predators, high up in a tree.

The peacock's train seems to be no hindrance at all in the forest; the male can take flight and dash through the trees or rise to the high canopy with ease if taken by surprise. Usually when danger threatens, however, peafowl prefer to run through the woodland— often one behind the other. Peahens with chicks are especially adept at dashing out of sight and making full use of every scrap of cover, such as a dip or hollow in the ground.

Peafowl are omnivorous and opportunistic, taking whatever food they can find. Groups of peafowl usually forage together. In the breeding season the groups may consist of a male with some females, although at other times the groups are made up of females and young or bands of males. Peafowl often raid fields from nearby woodland to find food at dawn and dusk. Grain, leaves or shoots of crops, berries, wild figs, and other fruits are eaten with relish. Great damage may be done to crops on farms by bands of peafowl.

hens. Early in the morning peafowl emerge from the forest, cautiously and quietly, to feed. Then they find a stream or waterhole for a drink. As they move, they do so with frequent pauses to look around, often with one foot lifted clear of the ground in a very elegant pose. Peafowl seem to walk with great care, attempting to remain silent among the dry, rustling leaf litter on the forest floor. They have big eyes

Trying to Impress

In the breeding season peacocks become solitary and aggressive. Each male establishes a territory, usually in a forest clearing, and calls loudly to advertise his presence. If another male tries to enter an established territory, a long and often violent battle may ensue. Within the territory the peacock has several special display sites, and here he waits until a group of females

↩ *A peacock throws his head back to make one of his loud, distinctive calls.*

approaches. The male now displays to the females by standing upright and spreading his train into a full, broad fan, tilted slightly forward. His wings droop and quiver, and the whole train vibrates, sometimes making a sizzling sound as the feathers rub together.

In this state the male stalks a female, hoping that she will be impressed enough to mate with him. During most of his energetic performance the females seem quite unimpressed—even dashing away from the male on occasions. Eventually, however, if the display has been successful, a female hesitates or crouches, and mating takes place.

The nests are well hidden in thick scrub, and each of the male's hens lays up to six (rarely eight) eggs in her own nest and then incubates them. The females and their chicks gather together with other families to form small parties living separately from the older males until the following breeding season.

Sacred and Safe

Because peafowl are sacred and revered in India, despite the damage they do to crops,

⤴ Female peafowl, or peahens, lack the long train of the male and have drabber plumage overall.

they are safe and secure at the moment, with no need for special protection. Peafowl are also kept as ornamental birds in many parts of the world, and they could become vital should future conservation efforts be required.

Choosy Hens

Hen peafowl appear to wander randomly between the displaying males in the communal display areas, but in fact they are assessing all the available peacocks very carefully and usually return to likely mates several times before deciding on the best male.

Studies of introduced, semicaptive populations have shown that hens are likely to mate with the male that has the most eye spots in his stunning train. Although the male with the best train is therefore likely to father most of the chicks, it is actually the female that makes the final choice, allowing only the male that she considers to be the fittest to mate with her. The male mates with as many hens as he can, and that gives him the chance of passing his genes to many successive generations. The female lays only one clutch of eggs, however, so she must try to mate with the biggest, fittest male she can find to ensure that she produces strong, healthy chicks.

Common Pheasant

Phasianus colchicus

A familiar bird of the countryside, the pheasant is also commonly seen hanging in the butcher's store in the fall. The cock pheasant is an eye-catching and handsome bird, with exquisite, glossy plumage.

Common name Common pheasant (pheasant, ring-necked pheasant)

Scientific name *Phasianus colchicus*

Family Phasianidae

Order Galliformes

Size Length: male 29.5–35 in (75–89 cm), female 21–24.5 in (53–62 cm); wingspan: 27.5–36 in (70–91.5 cm); weight: 1.3–4.4 lb (0.6–2 kg)

Key features Round-bodied, triangular-tailed, small-headed game bird; male with green head, coppery or golden-brown body with dark spots, green to orange-buff rump; female dull, spotted, shorter-tailed

Habits Lives socially; terrestrial except when roosting; noisy at dusk

Nesting Males mate with several hens; small nest on ground; 9–14 eggs; incubation 22 days; young fledge after 12 days; 1 brood

Voice Loud, crowing calls and abrupt "korr-kok"

Diet Fruits, seeds, and buds; occasionally insects and small reptiles, amphibians, and mammals

Habitat Woodland edge, overgrown riversides, edges of marshes, and farmland

Distribution Natural range across Central and eastern Asia, west to eastern Europe; introduced widely in other parts of Europe, North America, and Australasia

Status Common and secure in original range

THERE ARE 31 RECOGNIZED RACES, or subspecies, of the common pheasant and much variety even within those. In most areas matters are further complicated by captive-bred and released birds mixing with others of different appearance.

Colorful Bird

All races of common pheasant have a basically similar appearance. Mature males have a broad, disklike, bright red, fleshy wattle on the face and tiny "horns" on the back of the crown, a pale bill, and a glossy green head. The head looks black from a distance, but close up it is a beautiful emerald green with a blue-and-purple sheen. Many males have a white ring around the neck or a broader white patch; in Britain those without such markings are sometimes called "Old English" pheasants. The breast is usually dark, rich coppery-red or rust colored, while the back is paler, more golden-yellow, with or without large, pale spots. Bold, dark spots on the breast and flanks appear solid black unless seen close up, when they reveal a gloss of iridescent purple, lilac, and blue.

Long, drooping feathers on the rump form a kind of shawl of orange, brown, or pale green. Some races (in Russia and Afghanistan) have white wing coverts. This feature may be combined with or without a wide, white collar. The tail is long and stiff; and although it does not have the remarkably long, arched, or beautifully patterned appearance of the tails of the more exotic-looking Lady Amherst's (*Chrysolophus amherstiae*), golden (*C. pictus*), and Reeves' (*Syrmaticus reevesii*) pheasants, it is still eye-catching.

⊕ *During territorial disputes between male common pheasants, each leaps off the ground and tries to attack the other with his claws and spurs.*

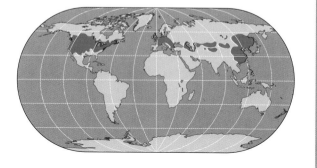

Females are pale buff-brown with spots of black. They have round, plain heads and shorter, but still elongated, spikelike tails that distinguish them from partidges.

Pheasants are rather short-legged birds, but more upstanding than the partridges, and more elegant and long-striding when walking on the ground. They are much more likely to run than to fly if disturbed. On the back of the leg is a short, stubby spur that males use for fighting.

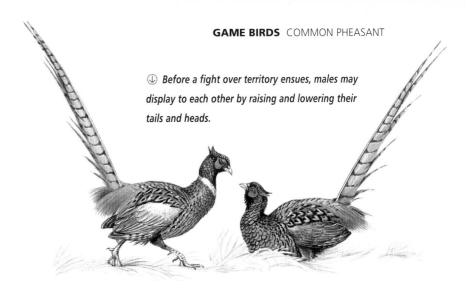

⊕ Before a fight over territory ensues, males may display to each other by raising and lowering their tails and heads.

Versatile Bill

The common pheasant has a stout, arched, but very short bill. It looks like a typical seed-eater's beak, but in fact it is able to perform a wider variety of functions. Like a farmyard chicken, a pheasant picks food from the ground with a series of rhythmic, fast, and accurate pecks, using its sinuous neck to dart the head forward and back. This same action can also stab and hammer small ground-dwelling animals such as voles, mice, or even young birds. Pheasants can be quite predatory; in southern England it is thought that common pheasants may be partly responsible for the decline in reptiles and amphibians, including slow worms and common lizards—a surprising conclusion for such a bird.

Pheasant Distribution

After widespread introduction as a bird hunted for sport, the range of the common pheasant stretches across the Canadian–U.S. border region and northern U.S. from the Pacific to the Atlantic, and from Britain and Ireland through the middle of Europe. The range continues eastward in a narrow, broken belt through Central Asia to China, Southeast Asia, and Taiwan. The native range is in this latter part, from Taiwan, China, and Vietnam, westward to the Caucasus Mountains in eastern Europe. The bird was also introduced to parts of Australasia.

There are millions of common pheasants in China—perhaps the densest population of the species anywhere away from localized

concentrations released for shooting in Europe.

Introductions have met with varying success. Even in the core of the European range, including Britain, numbers are constantly being reinforced by newly bred and released stock, most of which have little chance of long-term survival, although a few persist. In areas such as Australia introductions have failed altogether, but in New Zealand and much of the U.S. pheasants thrive.

Many of the wild-living pheasants in Britain are found in and around marshes, often within extensive reed beds provided there is woodland nearby. Most are released into scattered woods within lowland farmland. The marshy habitat, however, reflects the true nature of pheasant habitat in many places further east, since they prefer a mixture of woods, bushy areas, and riversides or more swampy lakeside fens. Common pheasants are also found on extensive plains with intense cultivation and on ranges of hills with scattered woods and farmland in the valleys; ideally, the birds prefer a mixture of terrain.

⊕ *This study of a calling male common pheasant shows clearly the iridescent colors, the red wattles, and the "horns" that characterize the bird. The "horns" are actually feathers.*

How Pheasants Live

Outside the spring breeding season common pheasants live in loose groups or sometimes more concentrated family parties. The groups spend the day foraging on the ground, sometimes flying from roosting areas in woodland to the open fields where they feed. In Europe and America they tend to be less mobile, wandering from the edge of a wood into open fields on foot and seldom flying very far. If alarmed, they will usually run, head and tail held high, into cover; they will only resort to flying if absolutely necessary. Released birds are usually very tame. Less tame birds will sometimes remain still until almost stepped on, at which point they will suddenly fly up underfoot with a great clatter of wings and noisy calls—an unwelcome test of an unsuspecting walker's nerves!

At dusk common pheasants move off to roost in trees—in which they are quite at home despite their apparently cumbersome long tails and general lack of mobility. There is usually a chorus of short, crowing calls from birds sorting out their roosting places and social hierarchy. Another call frequently heard is an abrupt, double note—"korr-kok!" It is immediately followed by a short, loud whirring sound made by a few rapid beats of the wings. Pheasants often call in response to loud noises, such as thunder or gunshot, and were frequently noticed calling during the early days of Concorde trials when the supersonic aircraft created sonic booms over land.

Pheasants are almost entirely vegetarian in the natural state, eating large grains and other seeds, as well as berries, fruits, buds, and leaves of many kinds, mostly picked from or close to the ground. Captive birds released into the wild have been found to eat a more varied diet, including reptiles and small mammals such as mice and voles.

Elaborate Mating Display

In the breeding season males become solitary and defend territories against other males. The males call to attract small groups of mature females, and usually from three to five hens gather at a male's territory.

Males then display to females with a ritualized performance designed to show off their glorious upper body colors and tails to best advantage. A male will attempt to corner a hen and head her off each time she tries to move away, by running from side to side and "shepherding" her back into place. At the same time, the male leans over sideways in an extravagant display, slightly spreading his wings and fanning his tail, while tilting over to display the maximum surface area to the hen. Like the female Indian peafowl, the female common pheasant at first appears entirely unimpressed with the male's display, but eventually mating takes place.

Once mated, the female lays her eggs in a shallow, grass-lined nest or almost bare hollow on the ground, well hidden under low vegetation. They are incubated by the hen alone for 22 days, although in many areas where pheasants have been introduced, incubation lasts between 23 and 25 days.

The downy chicks soon leave the nest but stay with their mother while she teaches them how to find food. They grow quickly and, in common with most game birds, develop their wing feathers unusually early, so that they are able to fly before they are fully grown.

Some Concerns

The wild common pheasant needs to be monitored with care; some races are scarce and threatened by habitat loss and excessive hunting. One race found in the Caucasus, for example, may number just two or three

Fast but Short Flights

Like other game birds, pheasants have large flight muscles. They provide the wings with short bursts of great power but quickly lose energy. Pheasants have quite short, broad wings that are ideally suited for maneuvering between trees when flying. The feathers at the tips of the wings are aerodynamically suited to fast acceleration. They can spread apart like the fingers of a hand, helping the wings obtain maximum lift when the bird needs to escape in a hurry. Pheasants take off in a sudden, rapid burst, creating a noisy "explosion" as they call and thrash their wings at the same moment. The birds soon change from powered flight to a long glide, however, and become exhausted quite quickly. A fleeing pheasant will usually fly a short distance, then glide to the ground and land "on the run," dashing off on foot to the nearest thick cover.

⊕ The drab plumage of a female pheasant helps her blend into the woodland while she incubates her eggs.

hundred pairs after a drastic decline caused by shooting and could easily become extinct. Other wild populations thrive and remain abundant despite large-scale killing. In areas where pheasants have been introduced for shooting, numbers are boosted every year by millions of young birds bred and released for sport.

Red Jungle Fowl

Gallus gallus

A glance at a picture of this bird, or a glimpse of the real thing, is enough to confirm that it is the wild ancestor of the domestic fowl.

Common name Red jungle fowl

Scientific name *Gallus gallus*

Family   Phasianidae

Order   Galliformes

Size Length: male 25.5–29.5 in (65–75 cm), female 16.5–18 in (42–46 cm); wingspan: 33.5–35.5 in (85–90 cm); weight: 1.1–3 lb (0.5–1.4 kg)

Key features Domestic chicken shape; male has striking colors—red comb and wattle, broad, thick shawl of orange-red and golden-buff; red-brown back and coppery rump; blue-black body and wings; long, arched, dark glossy green tail; female duller with mainly brown plumage but chestnut on head and neck

Habits   Lives in small groups on forest floor; generally shy and elusive

Nesting   Males mate with several hens; nest on ground; 5–6 eggs; incubation 18–20 days by the hen; young fledge after 14 days; 1 brood

Voice   Chickenlike clucking and crowing calls

Diet   Great variety of insects, seeds, shoots, and fruits; occasionally small reptiles

Habitat   Mostly forest, from sea level to 6,560 ft (2,000 m), but also other wooded and overgrown areas such as coastal mangroves and plantations

Distribution From Nepal, northeastern India, and Bangladesh, eastward to southeastern China, Vietnam, and Indonesia

Status   Locally common and secure

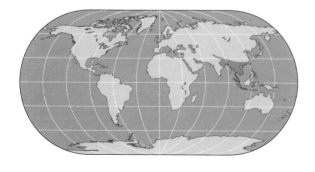

NOT ONLY IS THE RED jungle fowl the ancestor of the domestic chicken, it also looks almost identical to some of the varieties commonly kept on farms. The jungle fowl has a stout, deep body similar to a chicken. Males are solidly built, with short bills and short legs. The top of the head bears a red, fleshy fingered comb, and there is a hanging fleshy wattle under the chin. The area around the eye is bare red skin. The obvious feature distinguishing males from females even at a distance is the long, sickle-shaped tail—a bunch of curved, glossy, green-black feathers in an extravagant, sweeping arch.

Females are subtly and beautifully patterned. They are yellowish-brown on the head and neck, duller and darker on the body and rump, and black on the tail. Superimposed on this gradation from yellowish front to blackish rear are V-shaped streaks and spots—black on the paler parts and white on the back and wings. There is bare red skin on the forehead and around the eye. The female's tail is broad and rounded and is usually held cocked in the manner of most domestic hens.

A Life at the Forest Edge

The western boundary of the jungle fowl's range extends in a narrow belt into Nepal from Bangladesh and into northeastern India. Eastward it occupies most of the low-lying ground of Southeast Asia through Burma into Thailand and parts of southeastern China. The long Malaysian peninsula and a number of islands, including Java and Bali, are also inhabited by the red jungle fowl.

The whole of the bird's range is tropical or subtropical, and almost any bushy or wooded

Five races of red jungle fowl exist, varying in the precise shape and pattern of the wattles and other facial ornaments. There are also other variations such as the color of the feathery "shawl" around the neck. One race has a broad shawl of coppery-orange, and the feathers are broad and rounded. But the others have a yellower, spikier shawl of pointed feathers around the base of the neck.

Farmyard Crow

The call of the male red jungle fowl sounds like the familiar crowing call of a farmyard cockerel. The red jungle fowl has a wide range of calls, however, from the typical crow of the cock to the quiet clucks and "comfort noises" of the hen. They all have particular meanings, but some may have more than one function depending on the context in which they are used. The cock's loud, ringing, challenging crow is a territorial call used before dawn and during the day as he moves around his territory. However, the crow is also used by a male trying to impress a hen or seeking to express and confirm dominance over another male. It also serves to gather a feeding flock around the dominant male when he wishes to move elsewhere and as an "all clear" signal in an exposed area.

habitat from the coast up to about 6,560 feet (2,000 m) suits the jungle fowl. It does not thrive in dense rain forest, preferring forest edge or clearings where sunlight penetrates a little. Nor does it favor steep, mountainous, or heavily broken ground. In some areas—especially the southern part of the jungle fowl's range—habitat loss and degradation are causing a decline, since the bird needs both a variety of cover and suitable food plants.

Jungle fowl are terrestrial birds when feeding and resting during the day. However, they are very much at home in trees and fly up into the branches when disturbed or going to roost. Jungle fowl live in small groups, typically consisting of a cock with four or five hens. The group keeps well hidden in deep cover during the hottest parts of the day, but emerges into clearings and at the edge of the forest in the morning and evening. They are shy and rarely stay in view for long; indeed, they usually run into the forest at the first sign of danger.

In areas where jungle fowl have long been unmolested, they become bolder and live happily beside villages and farmsteads, picking food from around livestock and plowed ground. Jungle fowl are often seen on or around roads and tracks or in firebreaks through the forest. If taken by surprise, they will fly up with a clatter of wings and clucking calls, either to land in cover or to settle in a tree.

The cock crows at dawn before the birds emerge to feed and again at dusk as they find their roosting perches in trees or bamboo thickets. They also use noisy wingbeats to communicate with each other in the cover of the forest canopy. During the breeding season crowing calls are also made an hour or two before dawn, while it is still very dark. They are

⊕ *Red jungle fowl chicks develop quickly and are able to clamber about confidently within a few days of hatching.*

followed by a lengthy lull before the usual noisy wakeup period as the birds descend from the trees. In the daytime calls are given from raised perches, such as an anthill or fallen log.

The way that a jungle fowl finds and picks up its food will be familiar to anyone who has watched a chicken. It uses the same steady walk, leaning forward and exploring possible food items by pecking at them with a precise, rapid, rhythmic action. Anything edible is swallowed, and other items are discarded. Ants, termites, beetles, and their larvae and eggs are eagerly eaten, while grasshoppers, small lizards, and even animal droppings may provide a meal. All kinds of seeds, grain, fruits and berries, shoots, and buds are also eaten. Bamboo seeds become abundant in season and then attract many jungle fowl to feed together. Jungle fowl take few commercially grown crops except rice.

Leaning Courtship

The cock jungle fowl has a display similar to that of the pheasant: drooping one wing, fanning his tail, and tilting over in the direction of the hen. He then runs around the hen in a semicircle, leaning over all the while in her direction, twisting back, and tilting over the other way for the reverse run. He will mate with each hen in his small group in succession.

The nest is a mere scrape on the ground, lined with grass, leaves, and bamboo, and well hidden on the forest floor. The eggs are incubated only by the hen; the male moves on to mate with another female at this time. The chicks usually stay with the hen until the winter. Sometimes the male remains to guard the last family he has produced as well.

Successes and Failures

Red jungle fowl have managed to survive in areas that have been transformed into rubber and oil palm plantations, and being moderately adaptable birds, their status seems to be secure. In certain areas, however, clearance of trees and scrub has made tracts of habitat unusable, and jungle fowl have consequently declined or disappeared. In some places, such as much of

Thailand, red jungle fowl continue to be common despite constant hunting and persecution, whereas in Indonesia a lack of protection both for the bird and its habitat has resulted in a rather rapid decline in numbers. In the future red jungle fowl are likely to remain common in the middle and northern parts of their range, but it is likely that they will gradually disappear from the southern fringes and isolated habitats.

⊕ *The jungle fowl was probably domesticated between 4,000 and 5,000 years ago. Today the domestic chicken is arguably the most valuable bird known to humans.*

Domestication

The domestic fowl may be descended from any one or more of the four jungle fowl species found wild in Southeast Asia, although the red jungle fowl is the most likely candidate. The domestic fowl was seen in India by 3200 B.C., in China by 1400 B.C., and reached

Egypt and Crete by 1500 B.C. It has been suggested that the domestic fowl reached the Americas after Columbus voyaged to the New World, but it probably arrived from Asia much earlier.

The domestic fowl was originally a bird of religious significance used in sacrifices to gods; it may have been held in such esteem long before being bred for eggs or meat. Cockfighting is an ancient tradition, too, and fighting cockerels were presumably bred before the chicken was widespread on human menus. The Greeks kept it for fighting, but the Romans developed it for food. Indeed, the Romans had a poultry industry, and several breeds were developed. It collapsed with the fall of the Roman Empire, and large-scale poultry farming disappeared from Europe until the nineteenth century.

There are some 37 modern breeds that produce food, together with 24 more that are kept for ornamental purposes. Several breeds are now rare and maintained by special interest groups. They vary greatly in size, shape, color, and pattern. Some cockerels in particular have a striking resemblance to the ancestral jungle fowl, but many breeds (especially smaller bantams) are almost unrecognizable—with more visual similarity to francolins (genus *Francolinus*), for example.

Common name Gray partridge

Scientific name *Perdix perdix*

Family	Phasianidae
Order	Galliformes

Size Length: 11.5–12 in (29–31 cm); wingspan: 18–19 in (46–48 cm); weight: 11–16 oz (312–454 g)

Key features Small, rounded bird; short-billed with rufous-orange face; streaked, brown back and barred flanks; pale, brownish legs

Habits Mostly found in small parties; pairs in spring; terrestrial; quite shy and secretive

Nesting Nest on ground, lined with leaves and grass; 15–17 eggs; incubation 23–25 days by the female; young fledge after 15 days; 1 brood

Voice Short, metallic calls when disturbed; rasping, creaky double note from territorial male

Diet Seeds, grain, leaves, and shoots; insects essential for young chicks

Habitat Arable fields and pastures with hedgerows and weedy banks, heaths, lower edges of moors, and dunes

Distribution Across Europe from Ireland eastward, south to northern Spain, north to southern tip of Scandinavia; east into Central Asia

Status Severe declines in most of its range, but still widespread and numerous

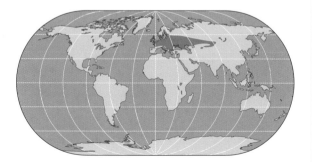

Gray Partridge

Perdix perdix

Calling repeatedly in spring, the gray partridge is a disembodied voice of farmland and heaths on warm, balmy evenings.

THE GRAY PARTRIDGE IS BIGGER than the quails but smaller than most grouse and pheasants. It is round-backed, short-tailed, and short-legged and moves with a rather shuffling, crouched walk. The plumage is brown above and gray below, with dark barring on the back and well-marked, creamy streaks. The brightest color is on the face, which is pale rusty-orange. There is also dark brown barring on the flanks.

On the lower breast there is a curved band of dark brown plumage; it is bigger on the male. Unlike the "red-legged" group of partidges, both the bill and legs of the gray partridge are dull and inconspicuously colored. In flight the gray partridge reveals short, broad, dark brown wings—held in a slight arch as it glides—and a short, rufous-sided tail.

Sounds of the Meadow

The gray partridge's core range is right across Europe from Ireland to the Black Sea and north to Finland, then in a narrowing band eastward to Kazakhstan and the tip of northwest China.

⊕ A male gray partridge calling. Intensive agriculture does not favor partridges, and the movement of eastern European countries into the European Union, with its agricultural subsidy system and constant push for greater efficiency, will inevitably cause partridge numbers to decline even further.

↑ Gray partridges dust-bathe in sand and soil to remove parasites from their skin and feathers. The movements are similar to those used by other birds bathing in water.

It is seldom found far north or in Iberia, although it is quite widespread in Italy and southeastern Europe and is found locally in the Middle East.

On a summer's evening the call of a gray partridge is a typical sound of the countryside. The bird's preferred habitat is green meadows and small cornfields with hedgerows or patches of rough ground with thorny bushes and tall, flowering herbs. Unfortunately, intensive farming has tended to replace such "wildlife friendly" places with huge, monotonous fields of sprayed crops that lack the wild plants, hedges, and field edges where a partridge can hide, rest, and feed.

Suitable grassland is still found on some dunes and around heaths, but the gray partridge prefers grass to heather and does not venture onto the higher moors. Gray partridges nevertheless survive in quite intensively cultivated areas, but always in greatly reduced numbers. They need variety, not monotony.

For most of the year gray partridges are social birds, living in coveys of a dozen or so. In the evening they roost together on the ground, and by day they spread out a little to feed but keep in close contact. If a predator is spotted, partridges crouch or move away through the vegetation. If taken by surprise or forced to make a move because an intruder gets too

close, they burst into the air with a sudden flurry and fly off, low and fast, with whirring wings and long, sweeping glides.

Adults eat mainly seeds, such as those from cereals or plants such as clover and pigweed. Many unripe grass seeds are snipped off by the birds in spring. In the 1930s it was established that weed seeds made up 31 percent of the diet in the fall in Britain, but by the 1970s that had fallen to 4 percent—a dramatic indication of the effects of intensive cultivation.

Furthermore, chicks are dependent on insect food for the first two weeks and need sawfly larvae (which eat cereal leaves but are sprayed as agricultural pests), beetles, and aphids. With far fewer of these insects around, gray partridges have a hard time unless special provision is made for them by encouraging grassy or even weedy field margins, where seed-bearing plants and insects can thrive.

Long Courtship

In spring males disperse and claim their separate territories, calling regularly to attract females and to announce ownership of their preferred patch. Males pair with hens weeks or even months before nesting, although they often break up during this period. Once the territory is established and the pair moves away from the covey, the bond becomes more stable. Even so, a male will sometimes also pair with a second female as well.

The nest is a typical game-bird scoop or depression in the ground with a little lining, but the clutch is unusually large even for this family of prolific egg-layers. As many as 24 eggs have been found, but 15 or so is more normal. If the first nest is destroyed or the eggs lost, a new clutch will be laid, invariably with fewer eggs.

The female does most or all of the incubation, but the male may be close by when the chicks leave the nest. They quickly learn to feed themselves. They also fly very early, when only about two weeks old, but are not fully grown for 14 weeks. By then many will have died—taken by predators or due to disease, starvation, or exposure in cold, wet springs.

Common name Willow grouse (willow ptarmigan, red grouse)

Scientific name *Lagopus lagopus*

Family	Tetraonidae
Order	Galliformes
Size	Length: 14–17 in (36–43 cm); wingspan: 16–18 in (41–46 cm); weight: 1.1–3.3 lb (0.5–1.5 kg)
Key features	Rounded, short-tailed, short-billed terrestrial bird with stiff, arched wings; rusty-brown; male with white belly, female barred paler beneath; wings white; white in winter; some races dark-winged and dark all year
Habits	Ground-living, secretive bird except when calling loudly in spring; lives in small coveys; flies low and fast if disturbed
Nesting	Nests on ground; 8–11 eggs; incubation 22 days; young fledge after 12–13 days; 1 brood
Voice	Crowing notes; abrupt, cackling call starts fast, then slows into clearly enunciated "go-bak, go-bak, go-bak"
Diet	Shoots, seeds, and berries; some insects in summer
Habitat	Arctic tundra and nearby areas of heath and moor; clearings in northern forest; some races on wide-open moorland
Distribution	Around Northern Hemisphere from western Alaska across northern Canada and arctic islands, and from Britain and Ireland and Scandinavia east through northern Europe and Asia to Pacific coast
Status	Common in most of its range; long-term decline in some areas

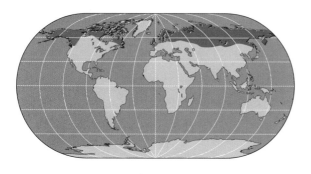

Willow Grouse

Lagopus lagopus

Short and stocky, superbly patterned, and attractive, the willow grouse is a northern bird of open habitats, from western moors to northern tundra.

THERE ARE NO FEWER THAN 19 races of the willow grouse, 13 of them in Europe and Asia. They fall into two main groups in Europe: the willow grouse, with white wings and all-white plumage in winter; and the red grouse of Britain and Ireland, with dark brown wings and year-round, all-brown plumage. The red grouse is sometimes considered as a separate species, but is generally thought to be a race of the willow grouse that has either lost, or failed to develop, a white winter coloration—presumably in response to less consistent winter snow cover.

Some races are rich red-brown with complex and beautiful spots and bars of cream, buff, and black, creating a variegated appearance. Others are more gray, with a pepper-and-salt scattering of fine black, white, and buff specks and bars, recalling the much grayer ptarmigan. Males have a small, fleshy, bright red wattle over the eye, and all have short, stout, thickly feathered white legs, which, in some countries, are coveted as "lucky charms" by people.

Range and Habitat

In the British Isles the high moorland of Ireland, western and northern England, and Scotland support scatterings of grouse where the habitat remains suitable, but they have declined in most places. Some grouse are found on lower moors, usually near windswept coasts. However, the soaking the birds get here during long spells of summer and fall rain and mist hardly favor their survival and breeding success.

The rest of the European population is more northerly—in Scandinavia and the Baltic states and east across Russia. The range then continues in a broad subarctic band right across

⊕ *Willow grouse begin to molt their reddish-brown plumage in the fall, replacing it with white plumage to help conceal them in the snow.*

SEE ALSO Game Birds **11**:44; Grouse, Sage **11**:70; Chicken, Prairie **11**:74; Birds of Prey **15**:8

Siberia to the Kamchatka Peninsula and Sakhalin. In the extreme north the bird is only a summer visitor.

This "grouse belt" is practically continuous on the Aleutian Islands and almost throughout Alaska and into northern British Columbia. Several of the northern Canadian islands support willow grouse on low ground in the summer; but this is a migratory population, and it moves to mainland Canada in the fall. Other races breed all around Hudson Bay and southeast to Newfoundland.

The low, shrubby growth of the Arctic tundra, which includes dwarf willows and birches as well as berry-bearing herbs, provides ideal conditions for grouse. Similar conditions are found further south on higher or exposed moors and hills, where there are also usually very extensive areas of heather. The best habitat consists of patches of tall, bushy heather for cover and nesting and short, new heather with succulent shoots for food.

between bouts of feeding. Rocky outcrops and hummocks provide higher perches from which males can call and challenge other grouse in spring. Willow grouse also live in forest glades with low, sparse bushes. Such a habitat is generally avoided by the British red grouse, which needs open ground but also occupies quite boggy places on peaty soils. In winter in Scandinavia and Canada the birds live in taller cover, such as thickets of willows and birch along streams and in broad valley floors.

Hidden in the Foliage

The young stay with their parents even when fully grown, sometimes joining other family groups or coveys. Together, they feed in low growth but usually remain crouched down and so are hardly visible from any distance. Should a predator such as a golden eagle (*Aquila chrysaetos*) appear, willow grouse will freeze, relying on their camouflage to remain unseen.

Willow grouse seldom move far and can often be approached quite closely. Suddenly, however, they will burst up out of the vegetation, either flying low over the moor or rising high to cross a broad valley. Willow grouse fly fast and powerfully, with outstretched necks and arched, slightly fingered wings, using bouts of

Willow grouse living in the north favor short plant growth that enables them to see above the vegetation as they stand up

Snow Tunnels

In deep snow a grouse digs a tunnel in which to conceal itself. Once inside, it fills the entrance to hide its presence. It is snug and warm in the tunnel, for the snow insulates the interior from the cold and the wind and helps prevent predators detecting the grouse. When it returns to a tunnel, the grouse flies there or drops down from a nearby tree to make sure that no tracks lead to it and give away the position to predators—although some are able to smell the grouse or, like the great gray owl (*Strix nebulosa*), hear it beneath the snow. Leaving the tunnel, the grouse breaks through its cover and pops out from the top, running or flying straight away. These vital tunnels are used mostly at night, but in very cold weather grouse also resort to them by day. In a temperature of −5° F (−21° C) up to 35 percent of a grouse's energy is saved by sheltering under the snow.

quick, whirring wingbeats interspersed with long glides.

Most races require willow for food. The leaves, buds, shoots, catkins, and seeds are all eaten by willow grouse. In Alaska willow forms more than 90 percent of a willow grouse's diet, but in Scandinavia much more birch is eaten. The diet depends on the other plants growing in the area. In fall and winter more berries are eaten, including short, leathery leaved shrubs such as bilberry and cowberry. British grouse are much more dependent on heather, eating new

shoots, leaves, buds, and seeds all year round, although in summer they eat insects, too. Young chicks also eat a lot of insects; but by the time they are three weeks old, they are already feeding almost entirely on heather. In winter, especially in severe weather, red grouse will take berries from hawthorn bushes.

Gamekeepers try to encourage higher numbers of grouse by providing piles of broken shell to add calcium to the diet. They regularly burn patches of heather to encourage a new growth of sweet, young shoots, but leave other areas to grow tall, tough, woody, and thick. These patches are little use for feeding grouse, but they give extra cover for nesting birds.

Singing from the Hilltop

Male willow grouse call from small hillocks, fallen logs, or stones, challenging other males with loud, echoing calls. They attract females and proclaim their territories with the calls. The call may be given in a short, rising song flight that ends in a long, low glide and a flurry of wingbeats as the bird lands.

Willow grouse do not display together at leks during mating, in contrast to other species such as black grouse (*Tetrao tetrix*), but remain separate and form monogamous pairs. If males meet, they bow at each other and then threaten with drooped wings, fanned tails, short chases, and erratic runs and leaps. The red wattles over their eyes also swell in

excitement; the dominant, or highest-ranking, males have the biggest red combs.

Each pair stays together for the summer, and the male often incubates the eggs and takes his part in caring for the young. The eggs are laid in a shallow scoop in the ground, lined sparsely with fine plants and hidden under thick herbs. After the eggs hatch, the downy young are soon active and are guarded by the parents as they begin to forage through the heather or herb layer. They can fly when under two weeks old and still quite small—a typical game-bird characteristic that allows the young to escape ground predators. Almost half the chicks die within a month or so. The survival rate depends greatly on the weather (cold, wet weather is disastrous for them) and the quality or quantity of food at critical times. The survivors are independent at about eight weeks; but if the food supply is poor in cold, wet summers, their parents may abandon them earlier.

Conservation

Red grouse in Britain have been intensively studied for decades because numbers have declined in most areas through a combination of disease and parasites (probably caused by poor-quality habitat), habitat loss (especially through overgrazing and overstocking with sheep), and predation. Managing the moors—in order to improve grouse numbers to create a surplus population that can then be hunted—is

difficult and expensive. In much of northern Europe willow grouse are still common, but declines have been noticed, probably due to climatic changes. There are marked fluctuations in the north, sometimes changing by as much as three or five times during ten-year periods.

In Canada willow grouse distribution is very patchy and occurs over huge areas of often rather unsuitable habitat, but locally they are much more common.

⊕ *The white winter plumage of the willow grouse camouflages it superbly in the snow.*

Prime Game Bird

Red grouse are not bred in captivity and released for shooting (unlike pheasants), but landowners often manage the bird's habitat to increase the numbers of young reared each summer. They then create a surplus "crop" for hunting. In Britain each spring a total of around 500,000 nesting grouse produce enough birds for hunters to shoot between 600,000 and 800,000 per year, although in the early 1900s as many as 2.5 million were shot annually. In Russia and Siberia about 8 million are shot each year, but fewer are shot in North America (some 94,000 in Alaska and 200,000 in Canada). In most areas shooting has had little long-term effect on numbers, but in a few places excessive hunting has been blamed for declines.

Sage Grouse

Centrocercus urophasianus

A bird of the American blue sage plains, the sage grouse remains relatively common in much of its range—unlike several of its North American relatives.

Common name Sage grouse

Scientific name *Centrocercus urophasianus*

Family Tetraonidae

Order Galliformes

Size Length: male 26–30 in (66–76 cm), female 19–23 in (48–58 cm); wingspan: 47 in (119 cm); weight: 3–7 lb (1.4–3.2 kg)

Key features Rather long, long-tailed grouse; short, dark bill; yellow wattle over eye; thickset head and neck; redddish-brown plumage with complex pattern; male black-and-white on head and neck, white ruff on breast, black plumage on belly; short legs

Habits Terrestrial; lives in small groups; males mostly separate from hens

Nesting Males display communally at leks; females nest on ground; 7–8 eggs; incubation 25–27 days; young fledge after 14–21 days; 1 brood

Voice Short, chickenlike, clucking calls when flushed

Diet Shoots and leaves of sagebrush, clover, and various herbaceous plants; young chicks require insects

Habitat Low, thick scrub and brush country, and dry grassland in plains and foothills

Distribution Widespread in western U.S and southwest Canada; range shrinking at edges

Status Locally common and secure; declining at fringe of range

THE WIDESPREAD SAGE GROUSE IS A LONG-TAILED, heavy-looking bird. It is much larger than the other grouse species that can be found nearby—the sharp-tailed (*Tympanuchus phasianellus*), ruffed (*Bonasa umbellus*), spruce (*Dendragapus canadensis*), and blue grouse (*D. obscurus*). They all have short or rounded, fanlike tails, whereas the male sage grouse has a longer, tapered tail with pointed, spiky central feathers normally held in a central point.

The male is eye-catching when seen close up, with a lot of black on the face and a white bib that extends into a densely feathered ruff around the lower breast. European grouse usually have fleshy red wattles above the eyes, but the sage grouse—like other North American species—has a rich, yellow eye wattle. Both males and females are beautifully patterned on the back and wings, with rich, reddish-brown feathers marked with black-edged white streaks. In flight the strikingly white underwing is revealed. The long tail lacks the white sides visible on the sharp-tailed grouse.

Birds of the Plains

Sage grouse are found from Washington and Alberta through southwestern Saskatchewan and North Dakota, to eastern California, Nevada, Utah, and Colorado. This area includes much of the Rockies, although the sage grouse is not really a mountain bird. Nevertheless, higher ground is occupied in summer but vacated in winter as the grouse move to lower ground. Such movements are not the true, seasonal migrations seen in many other species. They only take place when snow covers the topmost shoots of their staple food, sagebrush.

This forces the sage grouse to move on to find food elsewhere.

Previously, there were populations of the sage grouse in British Columbia, New Mexico, and Oklahoma. However, the bird is no longer found there, and some areas of California are also now devoid of the sage grouse.

The sage grouse prefers open plains and rolling hills with broad valleys and whalebacks, rather than steep ridges and sharp peaks. Such areas are generally very dry.

Keeping out of Sight

Sage grouse are usually fairly unobtrusive, especially in winter and also midsummer, when the small young hatch out. Sage grouse are beautifully camouflaged in the sagebrush and simply "melt away" in the vegetation or crouch and "freeze" motionless if disturbed, avoiding detection just by keeping still. They feed by day—in summer mostly early in the morning and again in the evening, with a lengthy rest during the middle of the day. In winter they have to feed throughout the short daylight

hours. During hot spells they keep under cover.

Males separate from the females in the fall and remain in small groups during the winter. They move to their display grounds in spring, as soon as the snow melts and before the hens arrive. Females and young live in small parties, tending to move farther away from the breeding areas than the larger males, which are more able to cope with severe weather.

Sagebrush is crucial to the sage grouse, as the bird's name might suggest. Sagebrush is a tough, aromatic plant. In winter its leaves make up almost the entire diet of the sage grouse. Other birds such as prairie chickens (*Tympanuchus cupido*) turn to seeds in winter, but they are avoided by sage grouse.

In summer more variety is possible, but sagebrush remains the favored food, although other herbaceous plants are also eaten. Like many young game birds, however, the young chicks require insect food for a fast intake of energy. Insects make up 60 percent of their food in the first week of life, but this gradually declines. By the time they are three months

⊕ *The female sage grouse is less striking than the male, with more uniform gray-brown plumage and a black belly patch. She also has a shorter tail.*

old, 95 percent of their diet is vegetable matter. Insect food (which forms a tiny percentage of the adult diet in summer, too) mostly consists of ants, small beetles, weevils, and grasshoppers.

Food is simply plucked from the growing plants as the grouse wander around on foot, using a chickenlike or pheasantlike quick peck of the stout, curved bill. This action is also ideal for clipping off the tips of shoots and leaves.

Breeding

In the spring males move to their leks—special display areas in open spaces, often on flat ground with rather short grass. When the females arrive, the males begin to display with great vigor. The finest males are selected by the hens for mating, so that their young have the best chance of survival by inheriting the same characteristics as their fathers.

Males are promiscuous, which means they mate with as many females as they can. Sage grouse are mature at one year, but most birds do not breed until they are two years old. Around 10 percent of the cock (male) birds at the display areas succeed in mating with about 90 percent of the hens.

The nest is a small depression in the ground, lined with a little grass and, inevitably, some sage leaves. Each hen lays her eggs, rarely as many as 15, and begins incubation. Hens leave their eggs just two or three times a day for short spells to find food, usually early in the morning and then again in the evening. They feed greedily while they can. Female sage grouse expel their unusually large, spiral-shaped droppings some distance from the nest in order to avoid the attention of predators.

While incubating, the female remains absolutely still; this is essential to make the very best use of the almost perfect camouflage coloration of her plumage. Of course, many predators are able to detect the hen and her eggs by scent, and despite the camouflage, predators take their toll of many clutches of eggs. As few as 25 percent of the clutches may hatch in some areas, but up to 60 percent may hatch in others. The chicks that hatch and

survive can fly within just one or two weeks—extraordinarily quickly—in order to get away from ground predators. This defense is little use if they are found by predatory birds, however.

Declining at the Edges

Sage grouse numbers are secure at present in their core range, but in places the population is declining and contracting. In 1952 there were some 150,000 adult birds. This figure had grown in the 1970s, when about 280,000 birds were shot each year by hunters. Hunting does not seem to affect the population overall, since the numbers of birds shot are roughly the same as the numbers that would die naturally through disease, starvation, and predation.

The future of the species is uncertain, however. In many areas sagebrush has been replaced by improved farmland, usually with irrigation or the use of extensive plowing or herbicide application to get rid of the ubiquitous plant. If this continues, the sage grouse will inevitably become more threatened.

➔ A male sage grouse displays at a lek. The impressive courtship ritual also includes intricate dance movements—all designed to impress females.

Putting on a Show

The sage grouse display is a remarkable sight—one of the most fascinating in a family of expert performers. Now the value of the long tail and heavy white ruff on the males is obvious. In a special display posture the tail is held erect and widely fanned, and the spiky feather tips separated in a broad, spiny-looking dish. The body is held steeply upright and taut, while the head is pulled back, with the thin, pointed black feathers at the back of the neck raised in a spindly ruff. The white neck and ruff are inflated and spread, with the feathers ruffled like the pile of a shaggy carpet. On each side of the breast an oval patch of bare, olive-green skin is exposed, while the wings are pushed forward, half opened, and then pushed backward and forward across the stiffly raised feathers of the ruff. This produces a loud brushing sound, while the bare skin patches are expanded and deflated, forming small air sacs and creating a loud bubbling and popping sound. All this time the male struts around with short, stiff, tiptoe steps in a performance that is spectacular but highly stereotyped and inflexible.

Common name Prairie chicken (greater prairie chicken)

Scientific name *Tympanuchus cupido*

Family	Tetraonidae
Order	Galliformes

Size Length: 16–18.5 in (41–47 cm); wingspan: 31.5 in (80 cm); weight: 1.7–2.2 lb (0.8–1 kg)

Key features Hump-backed, round-headed, short-legged grouse; yellow wattle over eye; closely mottled and barred plumage with black, white, rufous, and gray, giving an overall pale, marbled effect; some races more closely barred below

Habits Lives in small groups; males come together to display

Nesting Shallow scrape on ground, lined with feathers, grass, and leaves; 8–13 eggs; incubation 23–25 days; young fledge after 14–21 days; 1 brood

Voice Deep, booming "oo-loo-woo" sound in display

Diet Grains of cereal crops, acorns, leaves, and shoots; some insects

Habitat Originally open prairies mixed with oak woods—now modified into cereal prairies with patches of original grassland

Distribution Very local and fragmented in midwestern North America

Status Much reduced in numbers and range; 1 race perhaps secure through intensive conservation efforts, but even it is still declining in some areas

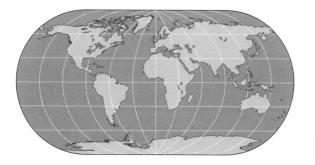

Prairie Chicken

Tympanuchus cupido

The prairie chicken is noted for its remarkable display. However, this bird is now difficult to see, since it is rare and declining in most of its former North American range.

AT A DISTANCE THE PRAIRIE chicken looks gray-brown, but closeup views reveal a complex and beautiful patterning of stronger colors that merge together into a pale, mottled effect. The underside is broadly and regularly barred with brown and buff. The rare and declining Texas race has a beautifully neat, tighter pattern of fine bars. The male has a big yellow wattle above the eye, and a black-and-white spotted shawl extends down from the back of the head to the base of the neck. In display it is raised in a remarkable upward-pointing spike behind the head, with the yellow wattles expanded and a big, bare, orange-yellow fleshy air sac inflated on each side of the neck.

Vanishing Races

One race of prairie chicken, now extinct in Louisiana, is found in Texas but has declined from 8,000 birds in 1937 to 2,000 in 1970 and to fewer than 1,000 now. Another race, at Martha's Vineyard, Massachusetts, became extinct in 1932. The remaining race is more common and is now found mainly from the Dakotas to Nebraska, Kansas, and Missouri after a long shrinkage of its range. Within the total range only tiny pockets are occupied, mostly because the habitat has become so unsuitable.

The prairie chicken was once the most common and widespread grouse of the great tall-grass prairies, where scattered oak provided patches of shelter, and periodic fires created more open spaces. The Texas race was found on sandy coastal plains that spread through forest clearings to the grass prairies inland and is still concentrated in what remains of such habitat.

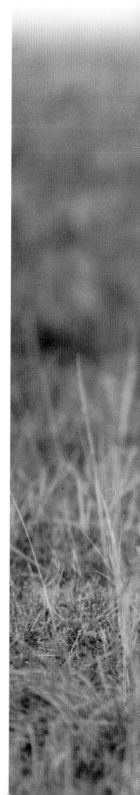

⤓ *During the breeding season male prairie chickens hold small territories within a display arena. Among displaying males there is much mock fighting and ritual. Real fighting often develops, too.*

Nowadays the prairie chicken has to feed on croplands of wheat, sorghum, corn, and rye, but it still needs access to patches of native prairie habitat. The remnant scraps of prairie provide places for prairie chickens to roost at night and for them to nest in; by day they move into fields to feed. They also need open areas in grassland, often on slightly higher ground, for their displays.

Like many other game birds, adults can survive on seeds and shoots, but young birds must eat insects. Grasshoppers are critical to their survival and also form a substantial part of the adult's diet in summer. For the rest of the year prairie chickens in the north now eat cultivated grain. Texas birds eat far fewer cultivated crops, under 10 percent of their diet being cereal grains. The leaves, shoots, buds, and seeds of native prairie plants are also eaten when they can be found.

Prairie chickens satisfy their hunger in quite short bouts of feeding. In winter they may feed for 80 minutes or so in the morning and for a similar period in the evening, resting for the rest of the day. The big cultivated grains provide the birds with plenty of energy, but in winter conserving it is important. At first, the arrival of crops helped the birds, since they now had much more big grain to eat in winter; but this benefit was soon far outweighed by increased hunting and habitat loss.

Making an Impression

Males arrive at the display arenas in the dark and begin to defend their territories. The best territories are in the middle of the arena, for it is here that most females are concentrated. A displaying male enlarges his eye wattles, raises the feathers on the back of his neck, inflates his air sacs, droops his wings to the ground, and raises his tail, which is fanned, rattled, and abruptly snapped shut. He runs to other males and patters with a "foot-stamping" action on the ground. The air sacs on the neck create a deep, booming "oo-loo-woo" sound.

When the hens approach, the males posture and prance and leap into the air, fluttering their wings and striking out with their beak and feet in an effort to rake across their opponent's plumage. The successful males mate with most of the hens. The chicks hatch with some of their wing feathers already partly grown, and they can soon fly a little way.

Common name Common turkey (wild turkey)

Scientific name *Meleagris gallopavo*

Family	Meleagrididae
Order	Galliformes

Size Length: male 43 in (110 cm), female 36 in (91 cm); weight: 9–22 lb (4–10 kg)

Key features Massive; fairly long-tailed and long-legged; fairly upright stance; slim, bare neck; small, bare head; glossy, blackish plumage; red coloration on head (females bluish); red legs

Habits Lives in groups on the ground by day; flies up to roost in trees at night

Nesting Nest on ground; 10–13 eggs; incubation 28 days by female; young fledge after 14–21 days; 1 brood

Voice Gobbling sound made by male

Diet Acorns, seeds, fruits, leaves, shoots, and roots; young eat insects

Habitat Bushy grassland and cultivated ground near forests; temperate regions south to subtropics

Distribution Widespread in North America from Pacific to Atlantic coasts, north to Ontario and south to Florida and Mexico

Status Recent increase after long decline, now numerous; often restocked and reintroduced into parts of range from which it had been lost

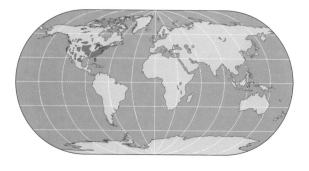

GROUND BIRDS

Common Turkey

Meleagris gallopavo

Like the jungle fowl, the common turkey is the ancestor of one of the world's most widespread and abundant domestic animals. It is difficult to believe that this ubiquitous bird was nearly decimated in the wild.

A COMMON TURKEY IS ONE of the easiest birds in the world to recognize because it looks and sounds very much like the turkey of the farmyard. A true wild turkey is, however, a little smaller and slimmer than the domesticated one. Both sexes have an almost bare head and upper neck, although the female's is bluish, with more bristly feathers on the nape. The male has brighter red skin and a bigger, loose, fleshy wattle under the throat. Both sexes have small, red, upright wattles over the bill, big, dark eyes, and prominent ear openings.

The body plumage is essentially blackish with broad, intensely black bands across the feather tips. The rest of the feathers have a purple-brown, copper, and green iridescence. Eastern birds have broad, chestnut tips on the upper tail coverts; in birds of more western areas these feathers are tipped dull white. The wing feathers are browner, with fine, pale buff or whitish bars on the quills. The breast of the male bears a drooping, brushlike tuft. He also has backward-pointing spurs on his shanks.

Fragmented Range

Common turkeys are found in a fragmented range that neatly fills the mainland U.S., with small extensions north and south. Most of the higher Rocky Mountain area is unoccupied, and there are many gaps in the vast cultivated

⬅ ⬆ During display the wattle of the male common turkey (left) becomes expanded (above).

76 SEE ALSO Game Birds **11:**44; Jungle Fowl, Red **11:**60

plains and southwestern deserts; but turkeys can now be found almost everywhere where they traditionally lived before America was colonized by Europeans. They were temporarily lost from many places but have since been transported back and restocked in these areas.

Turkeys need two elements in order to thrive: trees and grass. Trees are vital since they provide most of the bird's food and are also essential for safe roosting at night. Turkeys must roost off the ground so that they do not become victims of mammalian predators. Grass gives cover for nesting and provides more food, but importantly, it is a source of insects, which young turkeys need in their first few weeks.

In North America the ideal turkey habitat is open forest with grassy clearings or glades with sufficient sunlight penetrating the loose canopy to allow a tall, grassy, and herbaceous ground layer to develop. Dense forest bisected with logging tracks and other openings—allowing grass to invade—also provides a habitat for common turkeys.

In summer the young turkeys forage in

⊕ A turkey preens itself in the snow. In cold conditions turkeys prefer to roost in big, spreading conifers because their wide branches create "pitched roofs" under which the birds can spend nights out of the snow and cold winds.

⊕ *The male turkey, known as a tom, is usually found with several females, except in the breeding season, when females are solitary until their chicks hatch. Females (in the background here) have similar plumage, although it is less glossy, and they lack the breast tuft of the male bird.*

open places for insect food; hay meadows and some crop fields are ideal for this, and a mixture of woodland and cropland is good turkey habitat, typically replacing the traditional forest with clearings that has mostly been lost. In cold winters forest habitat is more important to the turkey than open spaces; here there is more cover, less exposure to wind, rain, and snow, and usually more food.

Living Together

Turkeys are social birds. For most of the year they live in groups ranging from a few individuals to 20 or so. When nesting, the hen lives a solitary life for a few weeks, and the

young family may also remain separate from other turkeys until the early fall. Many families mix together, however, so there are parties of three or four mature females and their broods.

In winter turkeys may be forced to gather wherever food is available. There may be hundreds of birds at exceptionally good feeding sites, but a strong social structure develops, and a good deal of pecking and jousting ensures that a hierarchy is maintained.

By late winter young males will leave the family groups and go off together. They may not become mature early enough to breed in their first year and, in any case, will no doubt be lower in the social hierarchy than older

males, so they wait a year before displaying and seeking hens.

Turkeys are true omnivores, eating what they can find. Studies of turkeys have revealed 100 different types of food being taken at one time in a single area. In summer they eat a great deal of foliage—herbaceous leaves and grasses found in the forest glades or along the edges of fields and clearings. Flowers, buds, fruit, and seeds are also taken from plants.

Some seeds and larger items such as acorns and fleshy roots are picked up from the ground or dug from the soil. Turkeys have powerful feet that can dig and scratch through thick leaf litter in a forest with ease. The presence of turkeys in a wood can often be detected by the scratched, scraped, and churned-up ground.

In some places spilled cereal grain in harvested fields is important food for turkeys. And when winter snow cover is too deep even for turkeys to dig through, they feed on buds in the tree canopy. Young turkeys, however, need a high-protein, energy-packed diet of insect food. For six weeks they eat only insects. Initially they survive on remnants of their egg yolk, but then eat 3,000 to 4,000 insects daily.

Calling from Cover

Early in the spring a familiar sound returns to American woods: the gobbling calls of male turkeys trying to attract hens. The vocal performance of the males is important, since the females may not be able to find the males in the dense forest cover without these sounds. Nevertheless, once the female is attracted within visual range, the male then puts on a show. He is determined to prove that he is the best male around, and that the female should choose him as the father of her young.

A displaying male droops his wings and raises his tail in a broad, beautifully banded fan. The pale or rufous tips on his tail feathers and upper tail coverts create a dramatic impression. He holds his head up and slightly back to

Inefficient Flyer

A male common turkey weighs between 9 and 22 pounds (4–10 kg). Turkeys have large, broad wings, but they are quite heavy birds, and their body-weight-to-wing-area ratio is also exceptionally high. This means that turkeys are not efficient flyers, and they use a lot of energy when flying. When disturbed, turkeys usually run away rather than fly. They escape uphill if they can, so that, if necessary, they can take off downhill and glide a considerable distance. They fly up with a sudden, powerful burst, as fast as 60 miles per hour (100 km/h), but must quickly settle into the long, downhill glide that takes them away with the least expenditure of energy. Flight from a treetop perch, going downhill, may last for 0.6 mile (1 km) or more, but much of this is on stiff, motionless wings.

enhance the colors of the blue and red skin against the black feathers of his back. If the female is ready to mate, the display is usually quite short. Females will be ready to nest early in the year if they have wintered well; but if a hen has suffered a bad winter and lost a lot of weight, she may not nest at all that year.

The hen makes a nest in a simple hollow on the ground, hidden under long grasses and herbs. She is isolated now, living away from the social group. She lays her eggs at the rate of

⬆ *A male common turkey fluffs up his feathers to help retain heat and prepares to ride out a snowstorm.*

one every 25 hours. When the sixth egg is laid, she starts incubation. This is a dangerous time, with foxes, skunks, and raccoons on the prowl. Fewer than half the nests are successful, but older birds fare better than young ones, suggesting that experience helps. Many female turkeys are caught on the nest, too, with eagles, coyotes, and bobcats frequently feasting on fresh turkey meat.

The chicks are able to run around soon after hatching. Although the mother stays with them, many chicks are caught by predators or die by accident or through hypothermia. Only about half the chicks survive the first three weeks of life.

Back from the Brink

Before Europeans reached America, wild turkey populations probably numbered tens of millions. Their forest-grassland habitat was abundant and widespread, and food plentiful. However, turkeys were good to eat and easy to shoot. Hundreds of thousands were killed, and by the late 1600s laws were passed in places in an effort to protect stocks. However, such laws were ignored or impossible to enforce. Turkeys rapidly disappeared from vast areas.

In addition to decimating turkey numbers, humans began to change the land, too. Turkey habitat was lost. Forest and open woodland on low ground was systematically felled—in the same way that the great prairie grasslands were extensively plowed.

This continued for centuries. By the 1940s there were only some 300,000 wild turkeys left. Only in the 1950s were hunting laws enforced and taxes from shooting used to help protect quarry species. Now turkeys were reared in captivity and released on a huge scale. Yet nearly all of these efforts failed to reestablish turkeys in the wild. What had gone wrong?

It seems that turkeys in the wild must be tough and competitive to survive. Yet it was difficult to breed tough and aggressive turkeys in captivity. Instead, captive birds were being released as tame, docile creatures, unable to cope with life in the wild. Young birds had no

Vital Brooding

A turkey hen looks after the chicks with no help from the male. The young chicks are at risk from predators and disease, but many also die from exposure if the weather is harsh. The hen often broods her chicks at night under her half-spread wings. For the first two weeks they are brooded on the ground, but later they scramble up into a tree, and the hen remains perched on a branch with her brood safely under her wings. The young soon become too large for this, however, and simply gather together on each side of the mother bird. Young chicks that remain protected beneath the hen's wings may survive cold and heavy rainfall, while those that are not may die. When the chicks are about eight weeks old, they will spread out into several trees at night, able to maintain their own temperature.

The Turkey Story

The curious thing about the turkey for European settlers was that they knew it as a domestic bird before they encountered it in the wild. They had turkeys in their farmyards back home, but presumably had little idea where they originated from. It was the Spanish who first brought turkeys back to Europe from their earliest explorations in Mexico. Turkeys were taken to Spain in 1491 and were common there by 1530. They reached Britain by 1541. In Britain, although other large birds were already called turkeys, the name was applied to the new domestic bird that supplied so much rich meat.

The name was then, naturally, given to the wild bird when it was eventually found living in eastern North America. It was also taken to America as part of the live food supply on ships in 1607. By then, of course, it has been important to native Americans for thousands of years. Along with deer, in the east the turkey was a prime source of food, while feathers were used in a host of ways: spurs made good arrowheads, and bones were useful for making a variety of tools. There is evidence of domestication of the turkey in New Mexico and Arizona as early as A.D. 500–700.

There is debate, however, about whether this was the first area of domestication and that turkeys were traded into Mexico and Central America, or whether the route was the reverse. It is quite likely that such a widespread and extremely useful bird was domesticated in several different places at different times. Domestic turkeys are now often white, and most commercially farmed birds are also white, with just a few farmyard turkey cocks remaining more or less like their wild ancestors. Millions of turkeys are raised every year in countries such as the U.S. and Britain, and in these countries the bird is second in popularity only to the domestic chicken.

chance to learn about survival from their elders, and most soon perished after release.

In the 1960s more effort was made to improve and protect the turkey's traditional forest habitats. At the same time, large areas of marginal farmland were allowed to develop as woodland—ideal for turkeys. Mixed dairy and arable farms made ideal habitats, too, provided the turkeys had some trees nearby.

Now wild turkeys, skilled in the ways of surviving in the natural world, were caught and used to restock the "new" habitats. Thousands of birds were translocated every year by the 1970s. Hunting was banned, and the turkeys were intensively studied so that biologists could learn more about their requirements.

By 1990 turkey numbers were back in excess of the three million mark—a stunning result that turned a mammoth and long-term decline into a great recovery. Although this is good news for the wild turkey, it is sad that many other species, including the closely related ocellated turkey (*Agriocharis ocellata*) of Central America, have been left to suffer and decline through hunting, illegal trade, and habitat loss.

Common name Mallee fowl

Scientific name *Leipoa ocellata*

Family   Megapodiidae

Order   Galliformes

Size Length: 23.5 in (60 cm); wingspan: 55 in (140 cm); weight: 3.3–4.4 lb (1.5–2 kg)

Key features Round-headed, short-necked, heavy-bodied ground bird; hump-backed and short-legged; gray head and neck; thin, black head crest; short, downcurved bill; black line down middle of the foreneck and chest; white underside; barred black, brown, and cream back and wings; strong, pale gray legs with thick toes

Habits   Generally solitary or in pairs; moves slowly and quietly through bushy areas and woodland; roosts in trees

Nesting   Extraordinary mound built for the eggs; 15–24 eggs; incubation 62–64 days; young fledge after 24 hours; 1 brood

Voice   Deep, triple booming note from male; also harsh, crowing call

Diet   Mostly seeds; also berries, shoots, and leaves

Habitat   Woodland and bushy areas with thick canopy above bushy ground layer

Distribution Southwestern, southern, and southeastern Australia

Status   Small numbers; declining and classified as Vulnerable

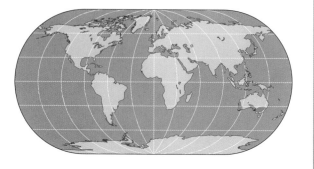

Mallee Fowl

Leipoa ocellata

There are several related mound-builders that lay eggs in heaps of earth and rely on the heat of the sun to incubate them, but the mallee fowl takes the technique a stage further.

IN A FAMILY OF VERY dark-colored species the mallee fowl is an usually pale bird. The upper side is an attractive mixture of chestnut, black, buff, and cream—the feathers being brown with a dark spot near the tip and spots and bars of cream around the fringes.

Scattered Range

There are three main areas of Australia where mallee fowl are found. The bird is fairly widespread in the southwestern corner of Western Australia, except where there is dense forest or a buildup of human habitation. Another area that supports mallee fowl is a central region along the south coast in South Australia. The third region cuts across the southeastern corner of Australia through New South Wales, including the mallee region inland from Adelaide.

The preferred habitat for mallee fowl is scrubby eucalypt woodlands on sandy soils, with almost complete cover at treetop level, but with open space beneath through which the birds can move. They are most common where a type of eucalyptus, called the dwarf mallee, is dominant, and where there is more than 12 inches (30 cm) of rain each year. Other good habitats include woodland with mulga (an acacia) and broombush. The critical element is an abundant supply of food within reach of the egg mound, which must be tended by the male for a long period, thus restricting him to a small area for most of the year.

Quiet and Wary

The big, slow-stepping, heavy mallee fowl has been described as "melancholy," since its demeanor suggests sadness. The bird is a quiet

⊕ *If the chicks are unfortunate enough to hatch when the male mallee fowl is around, they may simply get kicked and knocked around like lumps of earth; after months of ensuring their well-being, he has no interest in them at all once they are hatched.*

animal, wary and alert to danger and ready to freeze or move quietly away if approached. If it is taken by surprise, it will fly up and away over the treetops with a loud clattering of wings.

For most of the year the birds remain apart, even though the pair-bond may be strong. They mostly feed early and late in the day, and move into deep shade during the hottest hours. The birds often dust-bathe and laze in the sun. At night they fly up to roost safely in a tree.

Seeds are the most important food for mallee fowl, but a great variety of vegetable matter is eaten, including buds, flowers, shoots, roots, seedlings, and a large number of berries in season. Fungi are also eaten frequently. Beetles, cockroaches, ants, and spiders are also picked up from the ground, but it seems that they are taken by chance rather than deliberately sought out.

Amazing Egg Mounds

In late fall the male mallee fowl begins to build a special mound for the female's eggs. Related species lay eggs and cover them with soil—relying on the sun's heat to incubate them—but the mallee fowl is the only one that adds

⊕ The male mallee fowl digs a huge mound for incubating the eggs. This mound still has to be filled with the twigs and other vegetation that will slowly rot and produce heat for the developing eggs.

rotting vegetation to create extra heat. The male digs a pit 10 feet (3 m) across and 3 feet (1 m) deep, with soil heaped around the sides. With some assistance from his mate he fills the hole with leaf litter and thick twigs, raking it in with his feet and building up a mound more than 1.5 feet (0.5 m) high over the pit.

In the winter this heap is soaked by heavy rain. Then the birds dig a small egg pit in the top, line it with leaves and bark, and stir up the rotting material beneath before covering it with soil. The heat from the rotting plants will keep the eggs warm. Temperature control is vital; once the temperature reaches 86° F (30° C), the female lays her eggs several days apart.

The male remains by the mound, stirring and digging, opening it and recovering it, and maintaining the correct temperature. By late summer the heat of the sun threatens to cook the eggs unless they are sheltered, and the male opens the mound to allow it to cool by day but covers it each night. Once hatched, the chicks, already amazingly well developed, scramble out of the mound and must immediately fend for themselves.

Vulnerable Species

Mallee fowl are declining and already rare. In New South Wales and Victoria there are fewer than 1,750 pairs, but Western Australia has larger numbers. In eastern Australia around 80 percent of its former range is now devoid of mallee fowl—mainly because of habitat loss, overgrazing (which destroys habitat), fire, and introduced predators, especially European foxes.

The Bustard Family

Otididae

Long-legged, strong-billed, and broad-winged, bustards are ground birds that never perch off the ground. They have just three toes—ideal for walking but useless for gripping a perch. A bustard's small feet are not well designed for running either, and they are mostly slow-moving birds.

The "giant" bustards are huge—among the largest and heaviest flying birds in the world—but smaller species are not much bigger than a pheasant, and in flight they have a surprisingly ducklike appearance, with outstretched neck and rapid wingbeats. The bigger species fly very infrequently unless fleeing from predators,

⊕ **Carmine bee-eaters (Merops nubicus) ride on the backs of kori bustards and catch the insects disturbed by them.**

Family Otididae: 11 genera, 25 species, including:

Eupodotis	9 species, including black korhaan (*E. afra*); black-bellied bustard (*E. melanogaster*); Vigors' bustard (*E. vigorsii*); crested bustard (*E. ruficrista*)
Ardeotis	4 species, Australian bustard (*A. australis*); great Indian bustard (*A. nigriceps*); kori bustard (*A. kori*); Arabian bustard (*A. arabs*)
Neotis	4 species, including Nubian bustard (*N. nuba*)
Chlamydotis	1 species, houbara bustard (*C. undulata*)
Otis	1 species, great bustard (*O. tarda*)
Tetrax	1 species, little bustard (*T. tetrax*)

when they may need quite a long run to get airborne and then fly with a powerful, almost eaglelike action. The Arabian and great Indian bustards weigh about 22 pounds (10 kg); the kori bustard weighs up to 42 pounds (19 kg), and some great bustards tip the scales at 53 pounds (24 kg). Females are only about a third of the males' weight, although they are half to two-thirds their height and length.

Most bustards are brownish (some with a bright gingery hue), barred, spotted, and superbly well camouflaged. The females can be exceptionally hard to see if they keep still. In flight, though, many reveal startlingly black-and-white wings, and others have large areas of black plumage underneath the body.

Birds of Dry Places

Most bustards prefer wide open, grassy spaces with very few bushes and trees. In much of the world such places have been extensively developed for farming and housing, however, and bustards have suffered enormously as a result. Even planting hedgerows destroys bustard habitats, since they restrict the birds' views. As a result, several species are now extremely rare and threatened. Bustards are mostly birds of dry places, however, and they can survive in areas that have proved impossible to farm properly because they are too arid.

Bushy plains are fine for some species, however, so long as the vegetation does not close up the vista altogether. In such places bustards eat all kinds of plant material in addition to any small animals they can find and catch. Some species have been hunted for centuries, and the houbara bustard, especially, has been wiped out of vast areas by excessive hunting with falcons. Once a traditional activity, this has become a thoroughly well-organized hunt using advanced vehicles and support systems, dozens of falcons, and the most modern technology to ensure that few houbaras escape.

⊖ *A male black-bellied bustard displaying and revealing large areas of white on his outstretched wings. Males advertise their presence to females by calling from a mound before flying up with exaggerated wingbeats and gliding back to the ground on raised wings.*

Lifestyles

Most bustards can be found in flocks or at least small groups, although some, such as the kori bustard, are typically found singly or in pairs. In some species the males gather in groups while the females remain apart. Bustards are very quiet birds on the whole, although the little bustard makes a whistling noise in flight using a specialized wing feather, and some African species, such as Vigors' bustard, have loud, penetrating whistles.

Many bustards have dramatic prenuptial displays. Some African species, such as the black-bellied bustard and the crested bustard, engage in stunning aerial displays. Others, like the Australian bustard, perform exciting displays on the ground.

Bustards are long-lived birds, rearing few young, which are cared for only by the females. The males simply display and attract females, mate with them, and then move away. This reduces the threat of being killed by predators for both the males (which only need to protect themselves) and the females (which are far less conspicuous and therefore safer without the big, highly visible males drawing attention to them).

Australian Bustard

Ardeotis australis

One of several closely related bustards, the Australian bustard brings a flavor of the African plains to the wild parts of Australia.

Common name Australian bustard

Scientific name *Ardeotis australis*

Family Otididae

Order Gruiformes

Size Length: 35.5–47 in (90–119 cm); wingspan: 79 in (200 cm); weight: 6.6–17.6 lb (3–8 kg)

Key features Big, squarely built bustard with a stout bill, angular head, and long legs; black cap, gray neck, brown back, and white undersides

Habits Walks slowly over open ground or through tall grass; flies powerfully after short takeoff run; active after dark

Nesting Nests on bare ground; 1–2 eggs; incubation by female for 23–24 days; young fledge after about 28–35 days; 1 brood

Voice Hoarse, barking croaks, but mostly silent

Diet Shoots, leaves, fruit, buds, spiders, insects, small birds, rodents, and reptiles

Habitat Tussocky grassland, scrubby savanna, and open woodland

Distribution Australia and extreme southern Papua New Guinea

Status Remains common in some areas but declining or absent from parts of past range

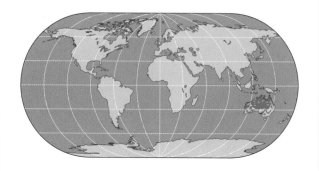

THIS HUGE BIRD IS AN IMPRESSIVE sight as it strides around purposefully on long, whitish legs with its head and pointed bill often slightly raised. It is remarkably similar to the great Indian bustard (*Ardeotis nigriceps*) and the kori bustard (*A. kori*) of Africa. However, it lacks the kori's small pointed crest but has a rounder black cap and a white streak over the eye. The neck and breast are pale gray—almost white—with the underside purer white and separated by a narrow, dark breastband. The whole upper side appears dark, dull brown when the bird is on the ground, but in flight a patch with black-and-white spots shows at the bend of the wing.

Wet and Dry Habitats

The Australian bustard is found over most of Australia apart from the southeastern corner and Tasmania. A small part of New Guinea has a healthy population. The bird usually inhabits open plains with scattered bushes in the dry season and taller, tussocky grass in the wet months. It nests in woodland edges and in hilly, bushy places near open grassland. In New Guinea it lives in more swampy areas.

Australian bustards usually keep to relatively small areas but may move on if prolonged drought makes life impossible, or if there is a plague of mice or grasshoppers, which attract them in larger numbers. Like other bustards, they remain firmly on the ground, never even resting in a bush or on a fence post. Like the kori bustard of the African plains, the Australian bustard can be seen from a great distance on open ground. However, a sitting or crouched bird—especially the female—is exceptionally difficult to locate.

⊕ An Australian bustard in typical pose. Although found over most of Australia, the core areas are the Northern Territory and Western Australia. The birds feed early and late in the day, when it is cooler. They may even be partly nocturnal.

 SEE ALSO Bustard Family, The **11**:84; Bustard, Great **11**:88

Australian bustards often feed at the edges of burned or burning grassland, snapping up rodents, reptiles, and large insects struggling to escape the flames. Much of the bird's food is vegetable matter that is plucked or snipped from the plants or picked up from the ground.

Puffed-up Mating Display

The male has a small, raised display area that is kept almost bare by his frequent marching over it. On this elevated spot he exaggerates the whiteness of his plumage by inflating his breast into a loose, hanging, puffy white pouch, that becomes so deeply extended it touches the ground. He raises his fanned tail over his back, stretches his head and bill upward, and flattens the tail forward onto his back. If a female approaches, he swings from side to side and spins around so that the inflated cheek pouches and the breast pouch shake and wobble. He then opens and closes his bill several times while making a series of ten or twelve deep booming or roaring sounds. If the female responds, the pair mate close by.

The female makes a shallow scrape in the ground for her eggs. After the eggs hatch, she looks after the chicks for several months, although they can fly after four or five weeks—well before they are fully grown.

Losing Ground

Once Australia was settled by Europeans, Australian bustards quickly declined through hunting. Farming and other development also put pressure on much of the wildlife. Introduced rabbits quickly became abundant and had a massive effect on the vegetation. The tussock grassland was largely bitten down to a smooth, tight mat unsuitable for bustards. The introduction of sheep was also disastrous for bustards, which could no longer find sufficient cover, food, or nest sites in the close-cropped grassland. As the human population increased and spread, building development pushed the birds from places that were once ideal for them.

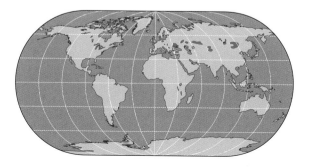

Great Bustard

Otis tarda

A huge bird, the male great bustard has a mating display that is one of the most remarkable sights among the birds of Europe.

GREAT BUSTARDS ARE HANDSOME AND impressive birds with great charisma. Males are huge, upstanding creatures with long, stout legs but typically small bustard feet. The plumage is a mixture of black-barred, tawny-brown feathers contrasting with white and pale gray feathers. There is a long, bristly "mustache" of whitish feathers sweeping backward on each side of the head from the base of the bill. Females are smaller and slighter, with smaller heads that lack the "whiskers," and they have less white on the open wing. Juveniles look similar but are a little browner with less gray on the head.

Scattered Ranges

There are various populations of great bustards in the world. Some birds breed in a small area of eastern Asia, from which they migrate southward into China each winter. Others occupy larger areas in Central and western Asia in summer, from which they move south into the arid areas of southwest Asia in winter. In Europe most great bustards are resident year-round in their breeding areas and can be found in very local areas scattered through Hungary, Russia, eastern Germany, Austria, the Czech Republic, and very locally in Spain and Portugal.

The ground-living great bustard requires wide open spaces, undisturbed by people and preferably with short or tussocky grass and no more than a few small, isolated clumps of trees. Such areas have become increasingly intensively cultivated; irrigation and the use of fertilizers and pesticides have turned vast areas of the bustard's former range into farmland that is no longer suitable for them.

Although some of the crops grown in these areas attract feeding bustards, the disturbance associated with their cultivation and harvesting

⊕ *Great bustards display mostly in March and April, from dawn to early morning and from late afternoon until dusk, sometimes with a resumption in the early hours on moonlit nights.*

Common name Great bustard

Scientific name *Otis tarda*

Family	Otididae
Order	Gruiformes
Size	Length: 29.5–41 in (75–104 cm); wingspan: 75–102 in (190–260 cm); weight: up to 53 lb (24 kg)
Key features	Massive bustard with boldly barred, tawny-brown upper side; mainly white underside and wings; male has gray head and orange-chestnut breastband
Habits	Lives in small groups or flocks in open spaces; mostly terrestrial but flying powerfully at times
Nesting	Nest is a scrape on the ground sparsely lined with grass; 2–3 eggs; incubation 21–28 days; young fledge after 30–35 days; 1 brood
Voice	Short, barking croaks, but mostly silent
Diet	Shoots, leaves, buds, and seeds; also insects, small reptiles, and a few small young birds
Habitat	Open grassland, semiarid steppe in lowlands and river valleys
Distribution	Widespread but extremely localized; Iberia eastward across mid-Europe into Central Asia and some parts of eastern Asia
Status	Rare and declining in most of its range; seriously threatened in much of its European distribution

is usually too much for the birds; they particularly avoid areas that frequently employ motor vehicles and noisy farming activities.

Life in the Flock

For most of the year great bustards are sociable birds. Even today, despite the long-term reduction in their numbers, hundreds of birds can sometimes be seen together in the fall and winter. These flocks usually consist of birds of one sex and similar age, such as old females or young males. Male birds tend to gather in ancient, traditional areas used by generations of bustards, but females wander more widely. The flocks may even be loosely associated with groups of mammals such as roe deer.

Like all bustards, great bustards are entirely terrestrial, never perching off the ground. At night they may roost on a ridge or some other good vantage point, but often they simply roost wherever they happen to be when it gets dark. They continue feeding after dark on nice nights, and males can be heard calling before dawn in spring. Even their full display has been observed in the bright light of a moon.

For most of the time great bustards are not territorial, and fighting among these powerful birds is kept to a minimum. This is achieved mostly by a strong social order or hierarchy. Young males often fight sporadically in spring, and this may help create a pecking order in the flocks. Old males rarely fight, however. Intruders, including other large birds such as cranes and even, rarely, humans, are sometimes greeted by a special aggressive display. The bustard lies almost flat with its head on the ground before making a sudden forward leap into a fierce attack.

Great bustards peck food from the ground in a typical graceful, easy action. They stalk forward with the head held low and the neck arched, ready for a sudden, quick lunge should a vole, lizard, or frog give itself away. Before it is swallowed, such prey will often be shaken in the bill until it is dead. Even larger animals may be tossed up and swallowed whole. Smaller prey such as insects are also picked up from the ground; grasshoppers, crickets, beetles, and weevils are typical items. Great bustards will also eat worms and woodlice, as well as a few birds' eggs and young birds from ground nests.

⊕ Fights lasting an hour or more may break out among rival males during the spring breeding season. Usually, one bird attempts to grasp another around the head with his bill and force it into submission.

Much of the birds' food, however, consists of plant matter. Many sorts of shoots, buds, flowers, ripe and unripe seeds, and fruits are taken. Clovers, dandelions, thistles, plantains, and various crucifers—the wild equivalents of cabbages—provide most of the diet.

Inside out Birds

The flocks of adult birds disperse in spring at the start of the breeding season. Most males now seek a special display area, where they spread out about 160 feet (49 m) apart. Males display in various places, however, and do not hold a special territory of their own. The performance begins with the "balloon display" and is accompanied by a deep, booming note. Males walk around with their tails raised and undertail coverts puffed out in a striking cushion of white.

This develops into a full display posture, with the head drawn right back to the rump and the throat grotesquely inflated into a feathery, white balloon. The whiskers are pushed up vertically in front of the face. The tail is brought forward flat onto the bird's back, while the male's wings are half opened and twisted over in a curious, "inside out" effect; at this moment it is sometimes hard to tell the front of the bird from the back, as the whole creature turns into an extravagant ball of white. For a few seconds the bustard stamps his feet, before slowly subsiding into his more normal shape; occasionally, however, a male may stay in his balloon pose for several minutes.

All this time, as the males wander around almost ignoring each other, the hens are attracted and gradually come closer. This may create more hostility and extra

The Future of the Great Bustard

The overall range of the great bustard has remained little changed in recent years, but within it numbers have plummeted, and breeding sites have shrunk into small, fragmented areas. There are several thousand birds still living in Spain and Portugal, but already large areas of suitable land are being altered by agricultural intensification. Semidesert lands in Spain are considered a challenge to be overcome by many farmers, who eagerly accept irrigation schemes and new reservoirs. Although these modifications enable them to grow crops such as sunflowers on semiarid steppe land, they destroy the habitat for the birds. The future of the great bustard in western Europe is therefore insecure. In eastern Europe plans for agricultural improvement in countries joining the European Union also leave little cause for optimism.

excitement among the males. A hen interested in a particular male will slowly approach him, often circling around rather shyly and nervously. At first the male may be nervous, too, and actually back away. Later in the season, however, they quickly mate, and the female then departs.

She makes a small, shallow scrape in the ground, lined with a few scraps of grass—probably accidentally trampled into the nest cup. The incubation period is quite variable in this species. When hatched, the chicks are cared for by the female alone. She feeds them when they are small, but they quickly learn to feed themselves. The chicks can fly within about 30 to 35 days and are able to live alone by the winter, although they may still be with the female in the following spring.

Conservation

The story of the great bustard is a sad one. The bird has long since gone from Britain (it last bred there in 1832), France (absent since 1863), most of Germany, Sweden, the Balkans, and large areas of Russia. Before this disappearance, however, the great bustard increased and spread greatly with the clearance of European forests. The range reached its peak around the end of the eighteenth century. The steppes and open grasslands were quickly replaced by arable land, however, and the bustards were soon in retreat, too.

⊕ The white undersides and predominantly white wings of the great bustard are clearly visible in flight.

Button Quails and Their Relatives

Turnicidae, Cariamidae, Rhynochetidae

The three families described here are visually very different. They are all grouped within the order Gruiformes, along with the cranes, rails, gallinules, the sunbittern, and bustards.

Button Quails

Button quails resemble Old World quails, or tiny partridges, although they are different enough to be placed in another family, the Turnicidae. Button quails have only three toes, lacking the small hind toe of most game birds. Females have strange, inflatable organs in the throat that help them create deep, booming calls. The organs are seen on calling birds as a small "balloon" under the neck feathers. A characteristic of the family is that the female takes on the usual male role—calling loudly to attract males, mating with them in succession, and laying several clutches of eggs that are each incubated by a different male. In most species the male incubates the eggs and looks after the chicks alone.

Button quails are small birds, some only 4.75 inches (12 cm) long and weighing as little as 1 ounce (28 g), while the biggest are only 9 inches (23 cm) long and 4.5 ounces (128 g) in weight. They are rounded, short-legged and small-headed, with short, slightly downcurved bills. Those that eat insects have slender bills, while the seed-eaters have thicker beaks—almost like finches.

Although very rounded in side view, button quails are slender-bodied. The shape and the three-toed feet are adaptations for slipping quietly through dense vegetation, particularly thick grass. It is hard to imagine why the hind toe is absent; it is so small on most game birds that it is not a hindrance, while other ground birds, such as larks (family Alaudidae), have long hind toes with very long, sharp claws.

Button quails creep quietly and secretively through vegetation. They have very short tails hidden by overlying wing feathers. Their wings are inconspicuous at rest but quite long when spread. Button quails fly more often at

Family Turnicidae: 2 genera, 16 species	
Turnix	15 species, including painted button quail (*T. varia*); Andalusian hemipode (*T. sylvatica*); barred button quail (*T. suscitator*); yellow-legged button quail (*T. tanki*)
Ortyxelos	1 species, quail plover (*O. meiffrenii*)
Family Cariamidae: 2 genera, 2 species	
Cariama	crested seriema (*C. cristata*)
Chunga	black-legged seriema (*C. burmeisteri*)
Family Rhynochetidae: 1 species	
Rhynochetos	kagu (*R. jubatus*)

⤒ *Two species of button quail: Andalusian hemipode or small button quail (1); barred button quail (2).*

 SEE ALSO Game Birds **11**:44; Bustard Family, The **11**:84; Seriema, Crested **11**:94; Kagu **11**:96; Cranes, Limpkin, and Rails **14**:82

night, using a weaker action that uses less energy over longer distances.

Button quails are found in most of Africa except in the Sahara and Namibian Deserts. One species, known as the Andalusian hemipode, originally lived in southern Spain and on some Mediterranean islands, but it may now be extinct in Europe. Another group occupies India, Bangladesh, most of Southeast Asia, the islands of Malaysia, and almost the whole of Australia.

Within these warm, tropical or subtropical regions are a range of habitats suitable for button quails. Some species live in open forest or woodland clearings. Others prefer drier places such as grassland with scattered bushes. Small species are found in extremely dry places because they do not need access to water. Some button quails live on arable land, especially if there are grassy meadows and mixed, leafy crops to provide food.

Button quails feed by day, but also before dawn or after dark for a time, eating seeds, buds, berries, spiders, and insects such as ants, beetles, weevils, grasshoppers, and caterpillars. Food is picked up from the ground, and some species feed in small groups with a characteristic

⊕ *Button quails, like the painted button quail shown here at its nest, are secretive birds that spend much of their time in cover. When disturbed they may fly away with a sudden, fast burst of whirring wings.*

"spinning" action, scratching circular patches on the ground. They use a similar technique to scrape out a shallow nest.

Seriemas

Seriemas are South American birds with a superficial resemblance to the secretary bird (*Sagittarius serpentarius*) of Africa, although they may be closely related to the bustards. They have long legs and tails, but small heads with short, hooked bills, and stride around on the ground searching for small prey.

Kagu

The kagu is a strange, isolated bird found on one Pacific island. It has features that give it an appearance somewhere between a button quail, a heron, and a rail. Examinations have revealed that the DNA of the kagu has similarities with the DNA of seriemas.

Crested Seriema

Cariama cristata

This unusual, long-legged bird of open landscapes is the wandering voice of the South American plains, where its loud, yapping calls of challenge and response can be heard each dawn.

Common name Crested seriema (red-legged seriema)

Scientific name *Cariama cristata*

Family Cariamidae

Order Gruiformes

Size Length: 29.5–35.5 in (75–90 cm); wingspan: 35.5 in (90 cm); weight: 3.3 lb (1.5 kg)

Key features Long-necked, long-tailed, and long-legged bird; short, red bill; wispy crest on forehead; dull, pale gray-brown; whiter below

Habits Solitary or in family groups; active by day on the ground; roosts in trees

Nesting Nests in tree made of sticks; 2 eggs; incubation 24–30 days; young (captive) fledge after 28 days; 1 brood

Voice Loud, repeated, yelping calls in long, variable series, audible over several miles, mostly around dawn

Diet Mostly insects and spiders; also small reptiles, amphibians, seeds, and leaves

Habitat Dry areas with tall grass, termite mounds, scattered bushes, or open woodland

Distribution Eastern South America

Status Small numbers throughout range but not threatened

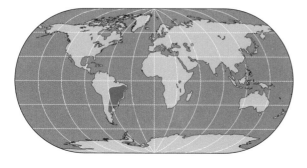

IN TERMS OF COLOR THE crested seriema is a dull bird. The plumage is pale gray-brown except for a white belly and vent, although the fanned tail shows wide, white corners, and the open wings reveal black-and-white bars. A broad, pale stripe curves over the pale eye, which is set in a patch of bare, blue skin. A peculiar, loose crest stands erect from the forehead. The short bill and long legs are salmon-pink to red. Young birds have gray legs and bills and barred upper parts.

➔ *A crested seriema in full cry. The calls are used to defend territory. Remarkably, young seriemas just two or three weeks old also join in the territorial proclamation.*

Voice in the Wilderness

Much more striking than the color of the bird is its voice. The yelping, wailing cries—given by a bird with its head bent back and bill wide open—have been likened to yapping dogs but have a musical quality, especially when one bird calls and is answered by another in a duet. Sometimes several birds call from low perches, such as bushes or termite mounds, their phrases overlapping in one long, varied, unbroken performance. There may even be several groups calling like this at a time, creating a rising and falling series of sounds from near and far all around the listener on the plains.

Should an intruder begin to call nearby, a seriema will leave its post and move toward its rival, calling as it goes. In some places captive or tame seriemas are kept in and around villages, and they are used to give loud, vocal warnings of approaching strangers.

Plains Hunter

Crested seriemas occupy much of the eastern side of South America, from close to the Atlantic coast to the edge of the Andes, and

from central Brazil in the north to northern Argentina in the south.

Much of this area is known as the Mato Grosso. Typical seriema habitats there include grassland dotted by thorn bushes that merge into open woodland at one extreme and bare, open ranchland at the other. The area ranges in elevation from close to sea level to 6,560 feet (2,000 m) in the hilly grassland areas.

This peculiar bird looks rather like the African secretary bird (*Sagittarius serpentarius*), and it behaves in a similar manner—walking steadily over open ground searching for food. It takes smaller food, however, principally grasshoppers, beetles, spiders, and even ants, with an occasional small rodent, frog, lizard, or snake. Usually one or two birds hunt a little way apart, but family parties may persist for some time and feed more or less together. Small items of food are snatched up in the bill, but larger prey may be beaten with the feet or held in the bill while being dashed against the ground before being broken up and swallowed.

Off-ground Nester

Although very much a ground bird, the crested seriema nests in a bush or tree, making a substantial structure of rough sticks and twigs, lined with leaves, earth, and cow dung. The eggs are incubated mainly by the hen. The chicks leave the nest after two weeks and obtain their adult plumage colors after four or five months.

Not Threatened

Crested seriemas are widely scattered over a large range, but nowhere are they common. In some areas farmers protect them because they eat snakes and rodents, but in other places they are killed for food. Their reputation as prolific snake-eaters is not really justified, and they are certainly not immune to snake venom as is sometimes popularly supposed.

Where arable farming has taken over open range land, the birds have declined, but massive deforestation in large areas has allowed them to increase in places.

Kagu

Rhynochetos jubatus

A unique bird of a South Pacific island, the flightless kagu is an unlikely shape for an inhabitant of the shady leaf litter of a subtropical forest.

Common name Kagu

Scientific name *Rhynochetos jubatus*

Family Rhynochetidae

Order Gruiformes

Size Length: 21.5 in (55 cm); wingspan: 30 in (76 cm); weight: 2 lb (0.9 kg)

Key features Round-bodied, thick-necked, long-billed bird; long, wispy head crest; body pale gray; bill and legs pale orange-red

Habits Resident in forest territory; feeds by day; generally solitary except when breeding

Nesting Simple ground nest; 1 egg; incubation 33–37 days; fledging period not recorded; 1 brood

Voice Pairs sing in duet with loud, crowing calls that carry at least 1.2 mi (2 km)

Diet Many small insects and other invertebrates—including worms pulled from the soil or dead leaves—plus a few lizards

Habitat Forest and moist, thick bush, from sea level to 4,590 ft (1,400 m)

Distribution A single island, New Caledonia, northeast of Australia

Status Endangered; under 500 birds in 1991

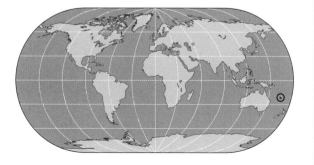

THE KAGU IS AN UNUSUAL looking bird, like a cross between a night heron and a kind of rail. It has a spiky bill, longish legs, a dumpy body, a short tail, and short, broad wings. It tends to stand very upright. The plumage is mostly pale gray, with a whitish head crest. The wings are barred with gray and white. The bird's large eyes are deep red and its bill and legs paler red.

Restricted Distribution

Only one small Pacific island, New Caledonia, is home to the kagu. Although essentially a ground bird where there is thick leaf litter beneath trees and shrubs, the kagu can actually forage in a variety of habitats wherever there is soft soil and a layer of dead leaves and open space through which it can move. It is usually associated with low rain forest but also survives in drier woodland at higher altitude inland.

Most food is picked up from beneath dead leaves or dug from the soil, and the bill is specially adapted with small flaps over the

⊕ *Confronted by an intruder on its territory, a kagu opens its wings and puhes them forward in a typical threat display intended to make the bird look larger.*

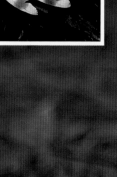

The kagu's long, bushy, drooping crest is spread wide and raised in a spiky fan as part of its territorial display. Kagus are monogamous and probably pair for life.

nostrils that keep out dirt. Kagus sometimes feed among rocks or find larvae in dead wood, and occasionally catch prey in the shallows of small pools. Mostly, however, they eat small items such as various grubs, millipedes, beetles, spiders, cockroaches, snails, and worms.

A feeding kagu moves stealthily on the forest floor, pausing to look and listen, and frequently stands on one leg while the other foot is raised or used to disturb prey. Once a small creature is seen, the bird darts forward and tries to snatch it up. If the first strike misses, it may have to dig it from beneath soil or dead wood using its strong, pointed bill. Worms are pulled out and swallowed whole, but big millipedes are usually broken into pieces before being swallowed.

Kagus are strictly territorial and use striking threat displays against each other. The wings are drooped and pushed forward, and the crest is raised. Similar postures are used against potential predators, but in this instance the wings are spread wide to reveal the striking bands of gray. If a chick is threatened by a predator, a parent will feign injury to distract it.

Slow Breeding Rate

The nest is a mere hollow in the dead leaves, with little or no lining. The adults gain weight before nesting but lose almost a quarter of their weight during the incubation period. Each bird incubates for about 24 hours at a time. Only one chick is reared each year by a pair that probably remains together until one dies. Kagus live a long time, perhaps up to 20 years, so a slow breeding rate is normal. On an island that is undisturbed this is a successful way of life; but as in the kagu's case, once alien predators have been introduced, it can be disastrous.

Saving the Kagu

Kagus were widespread throughout New Caledonia's forests until the arrival of Captain Cook in 1774. It was then that dogs were brought to the island and used by local people to hunt and kill kagus. Later, kagus were captured alive for sale to Europeans as pets. It is likely that direct predation on kagus by stray dogs has also contributed to a widespread and catastrophic decline. Cats, rats, and pigs may also prey on kagus, but the dog seems to be the main culprit. Because kagus lay just one egg each year, the population is simply unable to resist excessive predation of any kind.

Logging has wrecked much kagu habitat but, more importantly, brings more dogs into the habitat with the loggers. There are kagus in protected areas, but too few to make their future existence secure. Work by ornithological organizations will reveal more about the threats to this fascinating and unusual species, but a determined effort on behalf of the authorities to protect more habitat and reduce the dog menace is essential to the kagu's survival.

The Pratincole and Courser Family
Glareolidae

The pratincoles and coursers are rather unusual birds related to the waders and shorebirds in most ornithological family trees. However, there is some evidence—from examination of DNA and body tissues—pointing to a relationship with gulls and terns.

Pratincoles spend much time on the ground but feed mainly in the air, revealing unexpected agility and fluidity in their flight as well as a somewhat swallowlike shape. As such, they are "part-time" ground birds. Coursers, by contrast, are true ground birds in all aspects of their lifestyles, often preferring to run from danger (or crouch still) rather than fly. They can fly well, however, but behave much more like tiny bustards—feeding on the ground by walking or running and tilting forward to pick up food in the beak.

Old World Origins

This is an Old World group of species, mostly found in Africa and southern Asia, with offshoots in Australia. Only one species, the collared pratincole, is seen regularly in Europe. The black-winged pratincole is a rare visitor, while the oriental pratincole is merely an irregular vagrant outside its usual range. It seems likely that the group originated in Africa and spread northward and eastward over time. But unlike the thick-knees, it has no representative in the Americas. The spread of deserts in some regions may not help the coursers that live on desert fringes in dry, grassy, or scrubby regions, but changes in climate may produce some surprises. In recent years the cream-colored courser has, unexpectedly, not only visited Spain but also bred there.

Family Glareolidae: 5 genera, 17 species

Glareola	7 species, including collared pratincole (*G. pratincola*); rock pratincole (*G. nuchalis*); black-winged pratincole; (*G. nordmanni*); oriental pratincole (*G. maldivarum*); little pratincole (*G. lactea*)
Cursorius	4 species, Temminck's courser (*C. temminckii*); cream-colored courser (*C. cursor*); Burchell's courser (*C. rufus*); Indian courser (*C. coromandelicus*)
Rhinoptilus	4 species, including double-banded courser (*R. africanus*); bronze-winged courser (*R. chalcopterus*)
Pluvianus	1 species, Egyptian plover (*P. aegyptius*)
Stiltia	1 species, Australian pratincole (*S. isabella*)

⊕ *Representative species of pratincoles and coursers: Australian pratincole (1); double-banded courser (2); collared pratincole with raised wings, revealing how it derives its other common name—red-winged pratincole (3).*

Lifestyles

The typical pratincoles live near water most of the time, but not at the water's edge; they do not wade or swim. They prefer to rest on flat areas of dried-out mud or marsh grazed by animals such as sheep or cattle and to feed over such open ground rather than water. Having water nearby, though, undoubtedly helps pratincoles find an abundance of flying insects.

The rock pratincole of Africa, however, has a specialized habitat, being found on large, often wet, rocks in larger rivers (for example, the rocks above the Victoria Falls on the Zambezi River). The small pratincole of India and Southeast Asia also prefers rivers studded with rocks and sandbanks.

Coursers, by contrast, inhabit much drier areas, and some are, indeed, almost desert birds. The small Temminck's courser, widespread in Africa, and the double-banded courser of East and South Africa, inhabit grasslands. They are often found close to grazing herds of large mammals, running around on close-cropped turf. The bronze-winged courser, widely but thinly distributed in Africa south of the Sahara, is unusual in being strictly nocturnal. It migrates within Africa, moving northward after breeding.

The beautiful Egyptian plover is a little different from any of the others. Long since lost from Egypt, it is a remarkable bird of broad, lowland rivers mostly in West Africa, where it feeds on the shoreline and exposed sandbanks. It is credited with being one of the "crocodile birds" that remove particles of food from the teeth of crocodiles. Sadly, however, there is no reliable evidence that any bird species actually performs this task.

⊕ *In very hot conditions a Temminck's courser stands over its eggs to shade them, while ruffling its feathers, opening its bill, and fluttering its throat to keep itself cool.*

Cream-colored Courser

Cursorius cursor

An elegant, long-legged, and short-billed bird of semidesert and genuinely arid, hot desert lands, the cream-colored courser blends perfectly with its sandy habitat.

Common name Cream-colored courser

Scientific name *Cursorius cursor*

Family	Glareolidae
Order	Charadriiformes

Size Length: 7.5–8.5 in (19–22 cm); wingspan: 20–22.5 in (51–57 cm); weight: 3.5–5.5 oz (99–156 g)

Key features Rather rounded, but slim-necked, upright, small-headed bird; body pale, sandy-buff; black wingtips revealed only in flight; boldly striped head; long, whitish-gray legs

Habits Lives in small parties or pairs on open desert sand or among sparse shrubs and herbs; wholly terrestrial

Breeding Nests on ground in unlined depression; 2 eggs; incubation 18–19 days; young fledge after 30 days; 1 brood

Voice Short, simple, quiet notes uttered in flight

Diet Insects, especially beetles, grasshoppers, ants, and large flies; occasionally small reptiles

Habitat Sandy or stony deserts and dunes with sparse vegetation or a scattering of acacia trees

Distribution North Africa and Middle East; isolated patches along southern edge of Sahara Desert and East Africa; tiny populations on Atlantic islands (Cape Verdes, Canaries); winters just south of Sahara and in Arabia

Status May be increasing with southward spread of desert and grazing pressure; isolated outposts declining

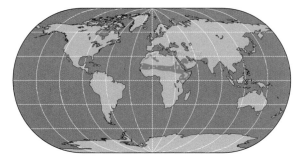

A TYPICAL COURSER IN SHAPE, with its short, curved bill, round head, slightly "waisted" neck, and roundish body, this is the palest and plainest of the family. The cream-colored courser is mostly sandy-buff, but whiter on the belly, and shows richer sandy-buff on the forehead and wing coverts. The rear crown is gray, forming a V-shape above parallel stripes of white and black behind the dark eyes. The outer wing and underwing are black.

⊙ *A cream-colored courser feeding in Israel. Most prey is swallowed whole without much effort, including large insects, scorpions, and the occasional lizard.*

Winter Arrivals

Around the southern fringe of the Sahara Desert this species is a year-round resident, but numbers increase in winter as breeding birds that spend only the summer months north of the Sahara and in the Middle East join the residents. More of Arabia is occupied in winter, too; surprisingly, this is a very localized breeding bird there, but it is locally quite numerous in Israel and Jordan. In winter some coursers also move from the Middle East into Pakistan.

The desert islands of the Cape Verdes have little more than 100 pairs, while those on Lanzarote and Fuerteventura in the Canary Islands are down to around 200 pairs after recent serious declines.

The bird's range also extends into Kenya, where a few wintering birds arriving from North Africa or the Middle East occupy very dry, barren places. However, the resident breeding birds can be found in much greener areas such as acacia bush and grassland. The resident birds, traditionally treated as a race (*littoralis*) of the cream-colored courser, have recently been considered the same species as Burchell's

SEE ALSO Pratincole and Courser Family, The **11**:98; Plover Family, The **13**:8

courser (*Cursorius rufus*), a bird that is otherwise found only in the extreme south of Africa. However, this race is smaller and grayer than other Burchell's coursers.

In winter other cream-colored coursers are found in such daunting areas as the Empty Quarter and Nafud Desert of Arabia and the Negev Desert of Israel.

In summer, in the north of Africa the birds prefer rather flat areas but can be found in huge, sweeping dunes or where sand alternates with stones and gravel. In much of Israel they breed in greener places where the desert breaks up into patches of shrubby or grassy vegetation. Such adaptability may become ever more important as the southern Sahara becomes drier, while in the north increasing areas are subject to development

and irrigation projects. In some places—especially Israel—the birds may even need to cope with some cultivation intruding on their great, wide open spaces if they are to survive.

Nothing to Drink

Although not nocturnal, cream-colored coursers tend to be active at dawn and dusk and avoid moving much in the heat of the day. They do not drink; indeed, most have no opportunity to do so, since there is usually no water available. What moisture they need must come from their insect food, and they have special nasal glands that enable them to expel excess salt accumulated from this diet. Living in such harsh places also

Hiding in the Sand

Coursers are beautiful birds, moving with a grace and elegance that suggest a great efficiency of action. In the demanding places they inhabit, energy conservation is of primary importance. The plumage pattern, paler below than above, is a classic example of "countershading." The light of the sun renders the upper parts very pale, while the pale color below cancels out the shadow and makes a courser on pale sand very hard to see when the sun is overhead. Colors become even paler as the feathers age, with pigments being bleached out by constant exposure to the sun. The pale legs are also difficult to see in strong sunlight and seem to separate the bird from the ground on which it stands; this also helps make it hard for any predator to notice a courser, because several of the usual visual clues are missing. Instead, there is simply a formless, colorless, floating shape that is hardly distinguishable from its surroundings.

means that food is likely to be patchy. Large areas have none; but where food is present, there may be enough to feed many birds. This problem, comparable to the one facing seed-eating finches such as linnets (*Carduelis cannabina*), is the usual situation that leads to birds feeding in flocks. Several birds together are more likely to find food than one, but there is no need to defend feeding territories if there is more food than one bird can eat. Cream-colored coursers are often found in groups of ten or a dozen, and in winter feeding parties sometimes consist of 20 or so birds.

Although a few locusts are caught in flight, the vast majority of a courser's food is picked from the ground. Either singly, in pairs, or in small groups, birds walk steadily forward, looking for prey. When food is around, they break into short, quick runs (they have no hind toe, a distinctive feature of so many active

Bill Types

Coursers and pratincoles have a smoothly arched bill of a type not seen in any other species of the suborder Charadrii. The cream-colored courser has a typical courser's bill: fairly long and used for digging into sand and soft soil for food, mainly small invertebrates. The bills of most of the coursers and the Egyptian plover (*Pluvianus aegyptius*) are similarly long and narrow. The Egyptian plover uses its bill to scrape sand over its eggs when it is disturbed and leaves the nest. This species and the three-banded courser (*Rhinoptilus cinctus*) incubate their eggs partially buried in sand, scooped up around and over the eggs with the bill. This sand may be wetted, helping to regulate the temperature of the eggs. In pratincoles, however, the bill is short but broad, and the gape is very wide. This is clearly an adaptation to help them catch flying insects.

ground birds) and stop to tip forward like plovers to snatch up their prey. Larvae are sometimes dug from the soil with the arched bill. Seeds are also eaten, but possibly they are picked up with insect prey.

Trying to Stay Cool

Coursers have quite poorly developed displays, with a circular display flight by the male or an upward climb on rapidly beating wings followed by a glide back to earth. The nest is simply a hollow scraped in the sand, maybe with a scattering of animal droppings around it.

Coursers are slow-breeding birds, unable to rear many chicks each year—a clear response to their arid and unproductive habitat. The sitting bird must endure extended exposure to great heat and direct sunlight. Some coursers reduce this exposure by taking short turns of some 15 to 20 minutes, but which the cream-colored courser survives for up to six hours at a time. Indeed, a problem for the courser is not so

ⓒ *A cream-colored courser attempts to shade both its chick and its unhatched egg from the searing heat of the sun. Coursers are monogamous, and both birds share the duties of incubation and raising the young.*

much how to keep its eggs warm, but how to keep them cool—direct heat from the fierce, tropical sun would soon kill the developing chicks inside.

Coursers often shade their eggs in the heat of the day by standing up and partly opening their wings. The courser also pants to cool itself down. When it becomes very hot—104° F (40° C) or more—the bird may settle again onto its eggs, rather than simply shade them, so that it can take heat from the eggs by body contact. This, however, risks dehydration—another of the many problems in the desert. During the very cold nights coursers must sit tightly on their eggs to keep them warm.

After the eggs hatch, the chicks quickly leave the nest with their parents, feeding themselves from the start. They are ready to breed by the following spring.

Living with Humans

Cream-colored coursers mainly inhabit terrain that suffers little disturbance by people. Coursers in the Canary Islands, however, breed next to intensively developing tourist resorts, and this brings all the attendant problems of disturbance. The disturbance is especially damaging when it includes the building of new roads, the "opening up" of new areas on the small islands, and the use of off-road vehicles for exploring the regions favored by the birds.

When noisy, fast vehicles such as these are used for recreational activities, they erode the habitat and disturb all the wildlife. Military exercises have added to the pressure on the habitats in recent years. However, until the emphasis shifts away from exploiting or destroying delicate habitats to one that nurtures and protects them, the birds will continue to be threatened. Protection, and its enforcement, are urgently required.

Elsewhere, though, cream-colored coursers are not faring so badly, and nests found in Spain have confirmed the spread of the species in some places in response to overgrazing by goats and perhaps increased desertification in response to climate change.

Lyrebirds and Scrub-birds
Menuridae, Atrichornithidae

Lyrebirds are extraordinary birds with tails up to 3 feet (1 m) long. Scrub-birds are no more than 10 inches (25 cm) in length altogether and do not look much like lyrebirds in any way. Why, then, are these two families linked?

The reasons are not obvious. The scrub-birds are thought to be ancient Australian species related to lyrebirds because they have a similar structure to their syrinx—the voice box in the throats of birds equivalent to the mammalian larynx. The families also share a second anatomical feature—neither has a wishbone (the fused clavicles in the chest).

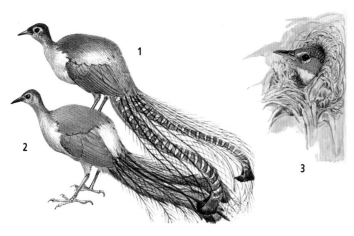

⊕ *Some lyrebirds and scrub-birds: male superb lyrebird (1) and Albert's lyrebird (2), showing tail variations; rufous scrub-bird at entrance to its woodpulp-lined nest (3).*

Familiy Menuridae: 1 genus, 2 species	
Menura	Albert's lyrebird (*M. alberti*); superb lyrebird (*M. novaehollandiae*)

Family Atrichornithidae: 1 genus, 2 species	
Atrichornis	rufous scrub-bird (*A. rufescens*); noisy scrub-bird (*A. clamosus*)

Lyrebirds

Lyrebirds are large songbirds. The males are slightly bigger than the females, and both sexes have long tails developed into special appendages. The male superb lyrebird has lateral tail feathers that are smoothly and elegantly curved, echoing the shape of a Greek lyre and giving the family its name.

Lyrebirds are famous for their songs. They have some of the most powerful, varied, and impressive songs in the bird world. The males' songs are also highly individual. One became famous overnight after an appearance in a television series on birds. Not only did the bird mimic several other species to perfection, but it also produced a high-fidelity reproduction of the sound of a camera, complete with a motor-drive unit! Then, sending a shudder down the spines of those who heard it, the lyrebird brilliantly imitated the sound of the buzzing chainsaw that was engaged in cutting down its already diminished habitat.

Lyrebirds are confined to eastern Australia. Albert's lyrebird is found only in the extreme south of Queensland and northeastern New South Wales. The superb lyrebird is found in Victoria and in the southeastern tip of Queensland. Remarkably, it is able to live anywhere from sea level to above the snow line on high peaks, in dense, temperate and subtropical rain forest, in swaths of tall ferns, and in overgrown, rocky gullies.

Male and female lyrebirds defend separate territories. The male attracts a female to his territory for the purpose of mating, but she then returns to nest in her own territory and rears just one chick.

In one or two places lyrebirds have become accustomed to people and are even fed by visitors, but everywhere else they are very shy and elusive.

Scrub-birds

The family Atrichornithidae contains only two species, and both of them are uncommon, shy, and rarely seen. Scientists believe that the family once had a much wider distribution, which is reflected now by relic populations isolated by climatic change.

The rufous scrub-bird is found in southern Queensland and New South Wales, inhabiting tangles of ferns and giant tussocks around fallen logs and stands of tall Antarctic beech. The noisy scrub-bird, by contrast, is found only in one tiny area of Western Australia. It likes dense, damp growth along streams, heathy headlands and adjacent swamps, and thickets of small eucalypts. The noisy scrub-bird is one of the world's rarest birds.

⊖ *The rufous scrub-bird is confined to the wetter parts of a few patches of rain forest on the eastern slopes of the Great Dividing Range from the middle of New South Wales up to southern Queensland in Australia. It is more numerous than its relative the noisy scrub-bird, but its numbers have decreased as a result of forest clearance.*

⬇ *A male Albert's lyrebird calling from the dense, subtropical forest it inhabits. All male lyrebirds sing to attract females and to warn off other males. The breeding season, and peak of singing activity, is in winter.*

Scrub-birds are not only rare, they are also elusive and very hard to see. Their small size and cryptic, drab plumage help them blend in with their surroundings. Because scrub-birds do not fly a great deal, live within a defined territory, and have powerful songs, tracking them down is not difficult—glimpsing the birds is the problem! Females are quiet, and mainly for this reason they are almost never seen at all. It seems that the male has a territory and that the female occupies a slightly separate or overlapping patch of habitat close by.

Common name Superb lyrebird

Scientific name *Menura novaehollandiae*

Family   Menuridae

Order   Passeriformes

Size Length: 34–39 in (86–99 cm); wingspan: 27–30 in (69–76 cm); weight: male 2.3 lb (1.1 kg), female 1.9 lb (0.9 kg)

Key features Dark, long-tailed, pheasantlike bird; plain brown body plumage with coppery wings

Habits   Lives singly or in pairs, deep in dense growth but sometimes seen crossing tracks or running along fallen logs; feeds on the ground; roosts high in trees

Nesting   Domed nest of sticks on ground or in tree; 1 egg; incubation by female for 42–57 days; young fledge after 43–50 days; 1 brood

Voice   High-pitched shriek of alarm; frequent loud, clear "bik" or "bilik"; both sexes sing, male more powerfully, and can mimic with great fidelity; basic song rich and mellow

Diet   Insects, worms, spiders, and other invertebrates scratched from soil and leaf litter

Habitat   Varied, including dense forest, rocky gullies, plantations, and gardens

Distribution Eastern Australia

Status   Scarce, declining locally but introduced into new sites

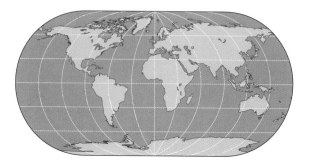

Superb Lyrebird

Menura novaehollandiae

One of the world's most individual birds, the male has characteristically broad, curved, outer tail feathers, creating a shape like the Greek lyre.

THE SUPERB LYREBIRD COMBINES A MEMORABLE song with a remarkable appearance. It is not the bird's coloration that is striking, however, but its shape. The head and body are pheasantlike, but with a more pointed bill, and the legs are long-toed and strong. The female has a very long, tapered, pointed tail, the slightly curved outer feathers of which are usually hidden.

The male, however, has three types of tail feather, with 16 feathers altogether. The middle 12 quills have long, lacy, silvery filaments instead of a stiff vane. The next pair is stiffer, long, and slim, and curves toward the tip. The outermost pair is broad, club-tipped, and sweepingly curved. They are marked with a dark and light "window" pattern along their length and are silvery below. The full tail may take between three and nine years to develop.

⊕ The superb lyrebird's outermost pair of tail feathers grow to 24 inches (61 cm) or more in length.

Tame and Tolerant

For such a rare and vulnerable bird, it may seem odd that the superb lyrebird can be found close to the city of Melbourne in Australia. Indeed, it has long been considered almost tame in Sherbrooke Forest Park. From this southern point it extends northward along the highlands into Queensland. The bird has also been introduced into Tasmania.

Fortunately, lyrebirds seem able to cope with some degree of interference and disturbance to their habitat and are even attracted to gardens and patches of freshly turned soil where they like to feed. Nevertheless, some forests in which they thrive are threatened, and in the long term they may face problems. They are, however, able to occupy both subtropical forest in the hot lowlands and cooler, temperate mountain woods, especially in some rugged, rocky terrain where trees and shrubs grow from deep gullies and chasms.

Mystery Bird

The lyrebird was first reported to Europeans in 1798 in a rugged area 60 miles (96.6 km) southwest of Sydney. No one was sure what kind of bird it was, and for a time names such as "native pheasant," "Botany Bay pheasant," and "New South Wales bird-of-paradise" were used. The term "lyrebird" was adopted during the 1820s.

Specimens were examined in London, England, as early as 1799 and descriptions published by 1802, together with reports that this bird was not only impressive when displaying, but was also a magnificent songster. This put an end to any idea that it might be a pheasant. When nests were found and proved to be made of sticks, with a domed roof of moss, and placed anywhere from the ground to a rock ledge or fork in a tree, the possibility that it was a game bird was also disproved.

Sadly, there followed a period of intensive slaughter; from 1815 until the end of the century many thousands of lyrebirds were ruthlessly killed for the sake of their tails. Although this traffic in plumes has been controlled, habitat loss continues, and pressures are increased by introduced cats and foxes.

Lyrebirds live most of their lives on the ground and can run well, but the value of their large, strong feet becomes clear when they start to feed. They turn over great heaps of leaf litter and dig deep into the soil in their search for worms, insects, spiders, and anything else they can find. Food items are snatched up with a rapid dart of the head.

Lyrebirds are generally shy and elusive, easily avoiding human detection in their densely forested or bushy habitat. They fly poorly, usually taking off downhill with long glides and a few heavy wingbeats.

Superb Display

It is not surprising that the superb lyrebird is often illustrated with its tail held upward and spread—in the classic chape of a lyre—for this is a dramatic spectacle. However, this is just a momentary phase in the male's display, and the tail is usually held flat, like a peacock's train.

In winter, when food is most abundant, the male scrapes up soil and stones from small clearings to form low mounds. He then uses the

⊖ *Superb lyrebirds fly upward through trees in a series of leaps and bounds from branch to branch. They roost high in the treetops out of reach of ground predators and glide down to the ground again each morning.*

SEE ALSO Scrub-bird, Noisy **11**:110; Kingfisher Family, The **14**:100

and singing finer and more varied songs than their rivals. What hen can fail to be impressed by a bird that produces more variety and greater perfection in his singing than his rivals? By choosing to mate with the male that has the best overall display, the female ensures that the next generation of young superb lyrebirds will inherit the characteristics of strength and vigor displayed by their father and will be best equipped for survival.

The hens move from male to male, assessing their potential as fathers for their young. Sometimes one, but often several, females establish their own territories around the fringe of a male territory. Each builds a nest and rears her own single chick alone, the male taking no part in incubation or feeding of the young. Young birds and adult females and males will, however, feed together in loose groups while the male is molting his tail feathers in spring and summer.

mounds when he displays. Fallen logs and stumps are also used for this purpose. Standing on the mound, he brings his tail forward above his back, shaking the central plumes in a shower of gleaming, silvery filaments. The outermost feathers are raised on either side, supported by the next pair of long, stiff plumes. With his tail pressed forward, he finally leaps backward and forward in time with his singing in a magnificent "dance."

Birds that look splendid in display usually have no need to sound particularly spectacular, and the best songsters generally rely on their voice to impress a mate, while keeping out of sight of predators. The lyrebird, exceptionally, excels at both visual and audible displays.

All the while he is displaying, the male also sings, producing some of the most piercing and pure of all bird sounds. His voice is probably the most powerful of all songbirds. A loud, repeated "bik" or "bilik" is often incorporated into the display, but the song is otherwise very variable between individual birds and areas, with obvious local "dialects" reinforced by mimicry of other residents. As well as imitating bird sounds, such as the raucous laughter of a kookaburra (genus *Dacelo*), lyrebirds can produce astonishingly accurate imitations of mechanical noises, from telephones to car alarms and car starter motors.

The advantage of being such a good mimic is not entirely clear, but probably lies in the fact that older, fitter, more experienced males can show their worth both by displaying longer tails

⬆ *Nest building, incubation, and care of the young are the sole responsibility of the female superb lyrebird.*

➡ *A female superb lyrebird takes feces and deposits them some distance from the nest to lessen the possibility of detection by predators.*

The Syrinx

Mammals produce sound through the vocal cords in the larynx at the base of the throat. In birds the larynx is small, has no vocal cords, and does little or nothing to produce vocal sounds. That role is taken over by the syrinx at the base of the windpipe. It has a resonating chamber, the tympanum, and several vibrating membranes controlled by a variable number of muscles that stretch and relax the membranes to create different qualities and pitch of sounds. There are seven types of syrinx in the bird world, varying from one with no musculature at all—as seen in the ostrich (*Struthio camelus*)—to those of the songbirds with up to nine pairs of muscles. Lyrebirds, despite the complexity and great power of their songs, share with the parrots a structure with three pairs of muscles.

Noisy Scrub-bird

Atrichornis clamosus

Small, elusive, dull brown, but with a remarkable voice, the noisy scrub-bird is one of the world's rarest and most restricted species and belongs to an ancient Australian bird family.

FOR MOST PEOPLE WHO ENCOUNTER it, the noisy scrub-bird is just a voice. The bird is rarely seen, although it may reveal its sharp, stout bill and long, broadly rounded, cocked tail.

Rare and Elusive

Until a recent program of translocation and reintroduction, Mt. Gardner, near Two People Bay in Western Australia, was the only known habitat of this species. Even so, it was thought for many years to be extinct before being rediscovered there in 1961.

Noisy scrub-birds are found in areas of low, heathy headlands dissected by streams and marshy places with rushes and sedges, various shrubs, and dense, stunted eucalypt thickets.

Studying scrub-birds is a frustrating occupation. When approached, they run like rats at great speed beneath the vegetation, probably through regularly used and familiar "runs." They live solitary lives except when a recently fledged chick remains for a short time with the hen.

Females are almost silent, perhaps giving short, single-syllable notes and contributing to a three-note contact call or alarm—"zip da dee." Otherwise, without even the voice as a clue to her presence, the female simply goes entirely unnoticed, keeping out of sight in dense cover.

Males are a little more obliging, however— at least they can be heard. The main song is powerful, ventriloquial, and like the lyrebird's song, extremely "one directional." The sound is projected like a long, straight beam, penetrating the thick cover from which the bird sings. The song, or call, of the male—"chip, chip, chip,

Common name Noisy scrub-bird

Scientific name *Atrichornis clamosus*

Family   Atrichornithidae

Order   Passeriformes

Size Length: 8–10 in (20–25.5 cm); wingspan: not recorded; weight: male 1.8 oz (51 g), female 1.2 oz (43 g)

Key features Sharp-billed, strong-legged, round-tailed bird with short wings; plumage rich brown above, whiter below; male with black patch on the white throat; tail—often fanned—has yellow-buff patch below; large, strong feet

Habits   Creeps on ground through dense undergrowth, rarely flying, using regular runs through vegetation

Nesting   Domed nest in rushes, close to ground; 1 egg; incubation 28–41 days; young fledge after 21–28 days; 1 brood

Voice   Descending series of sweet notes accelerate into explosive finish; male and female may call in duet

Diet   Insects and other small invertebrates

Habitat   Dense vegetation in damp places, swamps, sedge beds, and eucalypt thickets

Distribution Until recently confined to one site in Western Australia; now introduced to others

Status   1,500 individuals; Vulnerable

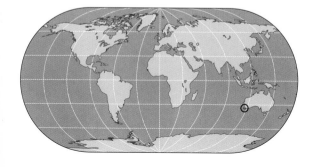

chip-ip-ip-ip"—begins with sweet, separate notes but quickly accelerates and increases in volume, to end in what has been described as "an ear-splitting and almost explosive crack." Although reluctant to reveal themselves, males seem to be curious and sometimes approach a human intruder, calling loudly. The first photograph of this species was taken when a bird briefly appeared in view after being attracted by a tape recording of its own song.

Cardboard-lined Nests

Breeding usually takes place in midwinter (June). The nest is an unusual structure, with material from decaying rush stems smeared to the inside while wet as a kind of plaster, creating a substance rather like cardboard. The nest is domed, made of rush stems, grasses, and leaves, and has a side entrance. It is placed up to 27.5 inches (70 cm) from the ground in a tangle of rushes or shrubs, on a small platform of leaves and stalks. The chick is ready to leave the nest after three or four weeks.

Fire Risk

Since their rediscovery noisy scrub-birds have been subject to intense conservation efforts, including capture and translocation to avoid all the birds being at one vulnerable site. Some of the translocation efforts have been successful, but others have been thwarted by rain and fire; once a small population suffers a setback, the birds' slow reproduction rate means it may never fully recover.

The original decline has been attributed to changes in aboriginal land management since the 1880s through the use of fire. Deliberate burning of the land is the chief threat to the species. At Mt. Taylor a translocated population was destroyed by fire in 1994. At Gardner Lake most of a population was lost after heavy rains in 1988 and 1991, and numbers never recovered. The current population Is estimated at 1,500 birds and is slowly increasing. For the moment the species is classified as Vulnerable rather than Critical thanks to the success achieved in expanding its tiny range.

⊕ The noisy scrub-bird was originally brought to the notice of the western world in 1842 and named by the famous ornithologist John Gould. The female probably has a small territory at the edge of the male's territory.

List of Orders and Families

Birds make up the class Aves, one of the groups of vertebrate animals. The class Aves is subdivided into a number of orders and families. Listed below are the orders and families of living birds—although not all ornithologists agree on a single, standard system of classification, and therefore some differences exist in other systems. The most common names of the birds within each family are given. Where a family is described in detail, the volume or volumes in which it appears are also listed.

Order Struthioniformes
FAMILY STRUTHIONIDAE — Ostrich *Volume 11*

Order Casuariiformes
FAMILY DROMAIIDAE — Emu *Volume 11*
FAMILY CASUARIIDAE — Cassowaries *Volume 11*

Order Rheiformes
FAMILY RHEIDAE — Rheas *Volume 11*

Order Apterygiformes
FAMILY APTERYGIDAE — Kiwis *Volume 11*

Order Tinamiformes
FAMILY TINAMIDAE — Tinamous *Volume 11*

Order Galliformes
FAMILY PHASIANIDAE — Pheasants, partridges, quails, peafowl *Volume 11*
FAMILY CRACIDAE — Guans, curassows *Volume 11*
FAMILY TETRAONIDAE — Grouse *Volume 11*
FAMILY MEGAPODIIDAE — Mallee fowl, brush turkey *Volume 11*
FAMILY NUMIDIDAE — Guinea fowl *Volume 11*
FAMILY MELEAGRIDIDAE — Turkeys *Volume 11*

Order Anseriformes
FAMILY ANATIDAE — Swans, geese, ducks *Volume 12, 14*
FAMILY ANHIMIDAE — Screamers

Order Gruiformes
FAMILY OTIDIDAE — Bustards *Volume 11*
FAMILY TURNICIDAE — Button quails, quail plover *Volume 11*
FAMILY CARIAMIDAE — Seriemas *Volume 11*
FAMILY RHYNOCHETIDAE — Kagu *Volume 11*
FAMILY GRUIDAE — Cranes *Volume 14*
FAMILY ARAMIDAE — Limpkin *Volume 14*
FAMILY RALLIDAE — Rails, coots *Volume 14*
FAMILY PSOPHIIDAE — Trumpeters *Volume 19*
FAMILY MESITORNITHIDAE — Mesites
FAMILY PEDIONOMIDAE — Plains wanderer
FAMILY HELIORNITHIDAE — Sungrebes
FAMILY EURYPYGIDAE — Sunbittern

Order Piciformes
FAMILY INDICATORIDAE — Honeyguides *Volume 17*
FAMILY GALBULIDAE — Jacamars *Volume 17*
FAMILY PICIDAE — Woodpeckers, wrynecks *Volume 18*
FAMILY BUCCONIDAE — Puffbirds *Volume 19*
FAMILY CAPITONIDAE — Barbets *Volume 19*
FAMILY RAMPHASTIDAE — Toucans, aracaris *Volume 19*

Order Coraciiformes
FAMILY ALCEDINIDAE — Kingfishers *Volume 14*
FAMILY CORACIIDAE — Rollers *Volume 15*
FAMILY BRACHYPTERACIIDAE — Ground-roller *Volume 15*
FAMILY LEPTOSOMATIDAE — Cuckoo-roller *Volume 15*
FAMILY MEROPIDAE — Bee-eaters *Volume 17*
FAMILY UPUPIDAE — Hoopoe *Volume 17*
FAMILY MOMOTIDAE — Motmots *Volume 19*
FAMILY TODIDAE — Todies *Volume 19*
FAMILY BUCORVIDAE — Ground-hornbills *Volume 19*
FAMILY BUCEROTIDAE — Hornbills *Volume 19*
FAMILY PHOENICULIDAE — Wood-hoopoes

Order Trogoniformes
FAMILY TROGONIDAE — Trogons, quetzals *Volume 19*

Order Coliiformes
FAMILY COLIIDAE — Mousebirds *Volume 20*

Order Cuculiformes
FAMILY MUSOPHAGIDAE — Turacos *Volume 16*
FAMILY CUCULIDAE — Cuckoos, coucals, roadrunners *Volume 20*
FAMILY OPISTHOCOMIDAE — Hoatzin *Volume 20*

Order Psittaciformes
FAMILY PSITTACIDAE — Parrots, parakeets, lories *Volume 16, 19, 20*
FAMILY CACATUIDAE — Cockatoos, cockatiel *Volume 16, 19*

Order Apodiformes
FAMILY APODIDAE — Swifts *Volume 15*
FAMILY HEMIPROCNIDAE — Tree swifts *Volume 15*
FAMILY TROCHILIDAE — Hummingbirds *Volume 16*

Order Strigiformes
FAMILY STRIGIDAE — Typical owls *Volume 15*
FAMILY TYTONIDAE — Barn owls, bay owls *Volume 15*

Order Caprimulgiformes
FAMILY CAPRIMULGIDAE — Nightjars, poorwills *Volume 15*
FAMILY PODARGIDAE — Frogmouths *Volume 15*
FAMILY NYCTIBIIDAE — Potoos *Volume 15*
FAMILY AEGOTHELIDAE — Owlet-nightjars *Volume 15*
FAMILY STEATORNITHIDAE — Oilbird *Volume 15*

Order Columbiformes
FAMILY COLUMBIDAE — Pigeons, doves *Volume 16*

Order Charadriiformes
FAMILY GLAREOLIDAE — Pratincoles, coursers *Volume 11*
FAMILY LARIDAE — Gulls, kittiwakes *Volume 12*
FAMILY STERNIDAE — Terns *Volume 12*
FAMILY STERCORARIIDAE — Skuas, jaegers *Volume 12*
FAMILY RYNCHOPIDAE — Skimmers *Volume 12*
FAMILY ALCIDAE — Auklets, guillemots, puffins, razorbill, dovekie *Volume 12*
FAMILY CHARADRIIDAE — Plovers, lapwings, wrybill *Volume 13*
FAMILY SCOLOPACIDAE — Sandpipers, snipes, curlews, godwits, woodcocks *Volume 13*
FAMILY RECURVIROSTRIDAE — Stilts, avocets *Volume 13*
FAMILY PHALAROPODIDAE — Phalaropes *Volume 13*
FAMILY BURHINIDAE — Thick-knees, dikkops *Volume 13*
FAMILY HAEMATOPODIDAE — Oystercatchers *Volume 13*
FAMILY CHIONIDAE — Sheathbills *Volume 13*
FAMILY DROMADIDAE — Crab plover *Volume 13*
FAMILY IBIDORHYNCHIDAE — Ibisbill *Volume 13*
FAMILY JACANIDAE — Jacanas *Volume 14*
FAMILY ROSTRATULIDAE — Painted snipes *Volume 14*
FAMILY THINOCORIDAE — Seedsnipes

Order Pteroclidiformes
FAMILY PTEROCLIDIDAE — Sandgrouse *Volume 16*

Order Falconiformes

FAMILY **PANDIONIDAE** — Osprey *Volume 15*
FAMILY **FALCONIDAE** — Falcons, kestrels, caracara *Volume 15*
FAMILY **ACCIPITRIDAE** — Hawks, eagles, buzzards, kites, Old World vultures *Volume 15, 20*
FAMILY **CATHARTIDAE** — New World vultures, condors *Volume 15, 20*
FAMILY **SAGITTARIIDAE** — Secretary bird *Volume 15, 20*

Order Podicipediformes

FAMILY **PODICIPEDIDAE** — Grebes *Volume 14*

Order Pelecaniformes

FAMILY **PELECANIDAE** — Pelicans *Volume 12*
FAMILY **SULIDAE** — Boobies, gannets *Volume 12*
FAMILY **PHAETHONTIDAE** — Tropicbirds *Volume 12*
FAMILY **PHALACROCORACIDAE** — Cormorants, shags *Volume 12*
FAMILY **FREGATIDAE** — Frigatebirds *Volume 12*
FAMILY **ANHINGIDAE** — Darters

Order Ciconiiformes

FAMILY **ARDEIDAE** — Herons, egrets, bitterns *Volume 14*
FAMILY **CICONIIDAE** — Storks *Volume 14*
FAMILY **THRESKIORNITHIDAE** — Ibises, spoonbills *Volume 14*
FAMILY **SCOPIDAE** — Hamerkop
FAMILY **BALAENICIPITIDAE** — Shoebill *Volume 14*
FAMILY **PHOENICOPTERIDAE** — Flamingos *Volume 14*

Order Sphenisciformes

FAMILY **SPHENISCIDAE** — Penguins *Volume 12*

Order Procellariiformes

FAMILY **DIOMEDEIDAE** — Albatrosses *Volume 12*
FAMILY **PROCELLARIIDAE** — Shearwaters, fulmars, petrels *Volume 12*
FAMILY **HYDROBATIDAE** — Storm-petrels *Volume 12*
FAMILY **PELECANOIDIDAE** — Diving-petrels *Volume 12*

Order Gaviiformes

FAMILY **GAVIIDAE** — Loons or divers *Volume 14*

Order Passeriformes

FAMILY **EURYLAIMIDAE** — Broadbills *Volume 20*
FAMILY **MENURIDAE** — Lyrebirds *Volume 11*
FAMILY **ATRICHORNITHIDAE** — Scrub-birds *Volume 11*
FAMILY **DENDROCOLAPTIDAE** — Woodcreepers *Volume 17*
FAMILY **FURNARIIDAE** — Ovenbirds, earthcreepers, horneros *Volume 20*
FAMILY **THAMNOPHILIDAE** — Antbirds, antshrikes *Volume 19*
FAMILY **FORMICARIIDAE** — Antpittas, antthrushes *Volume 19*
FAMILY **CONOPOPHAGIDAE** — Gnateaters
FAMILY **RHINOCRYPTIDAE** — Tapaculos
FAMILY **PIPRIDAE** — Manakins *Volume 19*
FAMILY **COTINGIDAE** — Cotingas, fruiteaters, umbrellabirds, cocks-of-the-rock *Volume 19*
FAMILY **TYRANNIDAE** — Tyrant flycatchers *Volume 17*
FAMILY **OXYRUNCIDAE** — Sharpbill
FAMILY **PHYTOTOMIDAE** — Plantcutters
FAMILY **PITTIDAE** — Pittas *Volume 17*
FAMILY **XENICIDAE** — New Zealand wrens
FAMILY **PHILEPITTIDAE** — Asities
FAMILY **ALAUDIDAE** — Larks *Volume 18*
FAMILY **HIRUNDINIDAE** — Swallows, martins *Volume 15*
FAMILY **MOTACILLIDAE** — Wagtails, pipits *Volume 17*
FAMILY **CAMPEPHAGIDAE** — Cuckooshrikes
FAMILY **PYCNONOTIDAE** — Bulbuls *Volume 16*
FAMILY **IRENIDAE** — Leafbirds
FAMILY **LANIIDAE** — Shrikes *Volume 15*

FAMILY **PRIONOPIDAE** — Helmet shrikes
FAMILY **VANGIDAE** — Vanga shrikes
FAMILY **BOMBYCILLIDAE** — Waxwings *Volume 18*
FAMILY **DULIDAE** — Palmchat
FAMILY **CINCLIDAE** — Dippers *Volume 14*
FAMILY **TROGLODYTIDAE** — Wrens *Volume 17*
FAMILY **MIMIDAE** — Mockingbirds, thrashers, catbirds *Volume 18*
FAMILY **PRUNELLIDAE** — Accentors *Volume 18*
FAMILY **TURDIDAE** — Thrushes *Volume 18*
FAMILY **TIMALIIDAE** — Babblers
FAMILY **SYLVIIDAE** — Old World warblers *Volume 17*
FAMILY **MUSCICAPIDAE** — Old World flycatchers *Volume 17*
FAMILY **PLATYSTEIRIDAE** — Old World flycatchers *Volume 17*
FAMILY **MONARCHIDAE** — Old World flycatchers *Volume 17*
FAMILY **ORTHONYCHIDAE** — Logrunners
FAMILY **ACANTHIZIDAE** — Australasian warblers
FAMILY **RHIPIDURIDAE** — Fantail flycatchers
FAMILY **PACHYCEPHALIDAE** — Thickheads
FAMILY **MALURIDAE** — Fairy-wrens *Volume 18*
FAMILY **PARADOXORNITHIDAE** — Parrotbills
FAMILY **PARIDAE** — Tits, chickadees *Volume 17*
FAMILY **AEGITHALIDAE** — Long-tailed tits *Volume 17*
FAMILY **REMIZIDAE** — Penduline tits
FAMILY **SITTIDAE** — Nuthatches *Volume 18*
FAMILY **CERTHIIDAE** — Treecreepers *Volume 17*
FAMILY **RHABDORNITHIDAE** — Philippine creepers
FAMILY **CLIMACTERIDAE** — Australasian treecreepers
FAMILY **ZOSTEROPIDAE** — White-eyes *Volume 18*
FAMILY **PARAMYTHIIDAE** — Flock berrypeckers *Volume 18*
FAMILY **DICAEIDAE** — Flowerpeckers
FAMILY **PARDALOTIDAE** — Pardalotes
FAMILY **NECTARINIIDAE** — Sunbirds, spiderhunters *Volume 19*
FAMILY **MELIPHAGIDAE** — Honeyeaters, spinebills *Volume 20*
FAMILY **EPHTHIANURIDAE** — Australian chats
FAMILY **EMBERIZIDAE** — Buntings, New World sparrows, cardinals, Galápagos finches *Volume 16, 20*
FAMILY **PARULIDAE** — New World warblers *Volume 17*
FAMILY **DREPANIDIDAE** — Hawaiian honeycreepers *Volume 20*
FAMILY **VIREONIDAE** — Vireos *Volume 17*
FAMILY **ICTERIDAE** — New World blackbirds, orioles *Volume 18*
FAMILY **FRINGILLIDAE** — Finches *Volume 16*
FAMILY **ESTRILDIDAE** — Waxbills *Volume 16*
FAMILY **PLOCEIDAE** — Weavers, sparrows, queleas *Volume 16*
FAMILY **STURNIDAE** — Starlings, mynas *Volume 18*
FAMILY **ORIOLIDAE** — Orioles, figbirds
FAMILY **DICRURIDAE** — Drongos *Volume 17*
FAMILY **CALLAEIDAE** — New Zealand wattlebirds *Volume 20*
FAMILY **CORCORACIDAE** — Australian mudnesters *Volume 20*
FAMILY **ARTAMIDAE** — Woodswallows, butcherbirds *Volume 20*
FAMILY **GRALLINIDAE** — Magpie-larks
FAMILY **CRACTICIDAE** — Bell magpies
FAMILY **PTILONORHYNCHIDAE** — Bowerbirds *Volume 19*
FAMILY **PARADISAEIDAE** — Birds of paradise *Volume 19*
FAMILY **CORVIDAE** — Crows, magpies, jays, ravens *Volume 18*

Glossary

Words in SMALL CAPITALS refer to other entries in the glossary.

Adaptation features of an animal that adjust it to its environment. NATURAL SELECTION favors the survival of individuals whose adaptations fit them to their surroundings better than other individuals

Adaptive radiation when a group of closely related animals (e.g., members of a FAMILY) have evolved differences from each other so that they occupy different NICHES

Adult a fully grown animal that has reached breeding age

Air sac thin-walled structure connected to the lungs of birds that aids respiration

Alarm call call given to warn others of the presence of a PREDATOR

Albinism abnormally white PLUMAGE (whole or partial) caused by lack of PIGMENT; true albinos also have red eyes, pink legs, and a pink beak

Allopreening the act of one bird PREENING another

Allospecies one of the SPECIES within a SUPERSPECIES

Allula group of several small, strong FEATHERS on leading edge of WING; used in flight to reduce turbulence and prevent stalling

Altricial refers to young that stay in the NEST until they are more or less full grown (as opposed to PRECOCIAL). See also NIDICOLOUS

Anisodactyl feet with three toes pointing forward and one pointing backward

Antarctic the continent, islands, sea, and ice that surround the South Pole

Anting highly specialized behavior in which a bird uses its BILL to apply ants to the PLUMAGE or lets ants invade its plumage, apparently in order to use the ants' acidic and antibiotic secretions to protect the plumage against PARASITES, fungal infection, and bacteria

Aquatic associated with or living in water

Arboreal associated with or living in trees

Arctic the polar region north of 66° 33' N

Avian pertaining to birds

Axillary the bird's "armpit"; FEATHERS in this region are called axillaries

Barb side branch from the central shaft of a FEATHER

Barbicel one of the tiny, hooklike structures on BARBULES

Barbule side branch from the BARB of a FEATHER

Beak see BILL

Bill the two MANDIBLES with which birds gather their food

Binocular vision the ability to look at an object with both eyes simultaneously, which greatly improves the ability to judge its distance, for example

Brackish slightly salty water (e.g., as found in estuaries where fresh water and seawater mix)

Breastbone bone separating the ribs, often deeply keeled to hold the strong flight muscles; also called the STERNUM

Breeding season entire cycle of reproductive activity from courtship and pair formation (and often establishment of TERRITORY) through nesting to independence of young

Brood group of young raised simultaneously by a pair (or several) birds: single-brooded (birds make only one nesting attempt each year, although they may have a replacement CLUTCH if the first is lost); double-brooded (birds breed twice or more each year); also triple-, multiple-brooded

Brood parasitism condition in which one SPECIES lays its eggs in the NEST of another, so that the young are raised by "parents" of a different species

Brood patch featherless area on the breast, with many blood vessels close to surface allowing more effective egg INCUBATION

Burrow tunnel excavated in soil where eggs and young are kept safely

Call short sounds made by birds to indicate danger, threaten intruders, or keep a group of birds together. See also SONG

Camouflage markings on PLUMAGE that aid concealment

Canopy fairly continuous (closed) or broken (open) layer in forests produced by the intermingling of branches of trees; the crowns of some trees project above the canopy and are known as emergents

Cap area of single color on top of head, sometimes extending to neck

Captive breeding program the breeding of a SPECIES in captivity with aim of controlled release into the wild

Carrion dead animal matter used as food by scavengers

Casque bony extension of the upper MANDIBLE

Cere fleshy covering on BILL where the upper MANDIBLE meets the face

Chick term applied to a bird from HATCHING to either FLEDGING or reaching sexual maturity

CITES Convention on International Trade in Endangered Species; an agreement between nations that restricts international trade to permitted levels through licensing and administrative controls; rare animals and plants are assigned to categories

Class a taxonomic level; all birds belong to the class Aves; the main levels of taxonomic hierarchy (in descending order) are: phylum, class, ORDER, FAMILY, GENUS, SPECIES

Claw sharp, pointed growth at end of a bird's toes; in the case of a young hoatzin also on the "thumb" and "first finger" of the wings

Cloud forest montane forest in TROPICAL or SUBTROPICAL areas with frequent low cloud cover, often at CANOPY height

Clutch the eggs laid in one breeding attempt

Colony group of animals gathered together for breeding

Comb fleshy protuberance on the top of a bird's head

Communal breeder SPECIES in which more than the two birds of a pair help in raising the young. See also COOPERATIVE BREEDING

Community all the plants and animals that live together in a HABITAT

Conservation preservation of the world's biological diversity through research, HABITAT and SPECIES management, and education

Contour feather FEATHER with largely firm and flat vanes; contrasts with DOWN, which is soft and loose

Convergent evolution independent acquisition of similar characters in EVOLUTION, as opposed to the possession of similar features by virtue of descent from a common ancestor

Cooperative breeding breeding system in which parents of young are assisted in the care of young by other ADULT or SUBADULT birds

Countershading form of protective CAMOUFLAGE in which areas exposed to light (upper parts) are dark, and areas normally shaded (underparts) are light

Coverts smaller FEATHERS that cover the WINGS and overlie the base of the large FLIGHT FEATHERS

Covey collective name for groups of birds, usually game birds

Crèche gathering of young birds, especially penguins and flamingos

Crepuscular active at twilight

Crest tuft of FEATHERS on top of a bird's head that can often be raised and flattened, especially during courtship DISPLAYS

Crop a thin-walled extension of the foregut used to store food; often used to carry food to the nest

Cryptic CAMOUFLAGED and difficult to see

Dabbling picking food from near the surface of water without diving, submerging, or UPENDING

Dawn chorus the peak of bird SONG around sunrise

Deforestation process of cutting down and removing trees for timber or to create open space for activities such as growing crops and grazing animals

Dimorphic literally "two forms"; usually used as "sexually dimorphic" (i.e., the two sexes differ in color or size)

Dispersal movements of animals, often as they reach maturity, away from their previous HOME RANGE

Displacement activity animal behavior in a particular situation, often during times of frustration, anxiety, or indecision; examples in birds include pulling at grass, BEAK wiping, or food pecking

Display any fairly conspicuous pattern of behavior that conveys specific information to others, usually to members of the same species; often associated with "courtship," but also in other activities (e.g., "distraction," "ecstatic," or "threat" displays)

Diurnal active during the day. See NOCTURNAL

DNA (deoxyribonucleic acid) the substance that makes up the main part of the chromosomes of all living things; contains the genetic code that is handed down from generation to generation

Domestication process of taming and breeding animals to provide help and useful products for humans

Down insulating FEATHERS with or without a small shaft and with long, fluffy BARBS; the first feather coat of CHICKS; in ADULTS down forms a layer beneath the main feathers

Duetting coordinated bouts of singing or calling by a mated pair or family group of birds

Dump-nesting laying of eggs by one female bird in the nest of another; generally occurs between birds of the same SPECIES

Dust-bathing squatting on the ground and using the WINGS, BILL, and feet to work "dust" (sand or fine, dry soil) into the FEATHERS to help condition PLUMAGE and remove external PARASITES; also known as dusting

Ear tuft bunch of long FEATHERS on the head, especially in owls, that the bird erects when excited or alarmed, but have nothing to do with the ears or hearing

Echolocation method of navigation and food capture that uses echoes from emitted sounds to warn of objects in the animal's path

Eclipse plumage drab, CAMOUFLAGING femalelike PLUMAGE acquired by males after a MOLT in the fall, when they lose their FLIGHT FEATHERS and become flightless and vulnerable for several weeks

Ecosystem the COMMUNITY of living organisms and their environment

Endangered species a SPECIES whose POPULATION has fallen to such a low level that it is at risk of EXTINCTION

Endemic found only in one small geographical area

Evolution development of living things by gradual changes in their characteristics as a result of MUTATION; involves ADAPTIVE RADIATION and NATURAL SELECTION

Extinction complete dying out of a SPECIES

Eye patch large area of contrastingly colored PLUMAGE surrounding each eye of some birds

Eye ring ring of contrastingly colored FEATHERS around each eye

Eye spot an eyelike pattern on PLUMAGE (e.g., the eye spots on the long tail COVERTS of male peacocks); also known as ocellus (*pl*: ocelli)

Eye stripe stripe of contrastingly colored FEATHERS running through each eye of a bird; one above the eye is called a supercilium

Family either a group of closely related SPECIES (e.g., penguins) or a pair of birds and their offspring. See also CLASS

Feather unique structure found only in the PLUMAGE of birds; a typical body (CONTOUR), wing, or tail feather consists of a central shaft, or rachis, and a vane, or web, bearing many horizontal branches, or BARBS, each bearing many BARBULES arranged so that they are linked together by tiny hooks (BARBICELS) forming a smooth surface; the lower, bare end of the shaft, inserted in the skin, is called the quill

Filoplume hairlike feather with a shaft but few or no BARBS

Fledge to grow feathers; also refers to the moment of flying at the end of the NESTING PERIOD, when young birds are more or less completely feathered

Fledging period time from HATCHING to FLEDGING

Fledgling recently fledged young bird

Flight feathers large WING FEATHERS composed of PRIMARY FEATHERS and SECONDARY FEATHERS

Flightless bird bird SPECIES that permanently lacks the power of flight (e.g., ostriches, emus, rheas, kiwis, penguins, flightless cormorant); all evolved from flying birds

Flock assemblage of birds, often involved in a coordinated activity

Food chain sequence in which one organism becomes food for another, which in turn is eaten by another

Frugivore an animal that eats mostly or entirely fruit

Gape width of an animal's open mouth

Gene basic unit of heredity enabling one generation to pass on characteristics to its offspring

Genus (pl. genera) group of closely related SPECIES. See CLASS

Gizzard muscular forepart of the stomach; often used for grinding food

Gonys bulge toward tip of the lower MANDIBLE; most visible in gulls

Grassland terrain with vegetation that is dominated by grasses, with few or no trees

Gregarious tendency to congregate into groups

Gular pouch extension of the fleshy area of the lower jaw and throat

Habitat place where an animal or plant lives

Hatching emergence of a CHICK from its egg

Hatchling young bird recently emerged from the egg

Heterodactyl toe arrangement in which the first and second toes point backward, and the third and fourth toes point forward; unique to the trogons (family Trogonidae)

Hibernation becoming inactive in winter, with lowered body temperature to save energy

Hierarchy establishment of superiority and rank among groups of animals, with dominant individuals at the top and subordinates lower down; subordinates often give way to higher ranking birds when feeding; among POLYGAMOUS SPECIES dominant males may mate with all available females; also called pecking order

Home range area in which an animal normally lives

Homing ability of some birds to find their way back to a regular ROOST from great distances; most familiar in pigeons

Hybrid offspring of a mating between animals of different SPECIES

Immature a bird that has not acquired its mature PLUMAGE

Incubation the act of incubating the egg or eggs (i.e., keeping them warm so that development is possible)

Incubation period time taken for eggs to develop from the start of INCUBATION to HATCHING

Indigenous living naturally in a region; NATIVE (not an introduced SPECIES)

Insectivore an animal that feeds on insects

Introduced decribes a species that has been brought from places where it occurs naturally to places where it has not previously occurred

Iridescence a glittering "rainbow" effect of green, blue, or bronze caused by the scattering of light from microscopic ridges on a bird's FEATHERS

Irruption sudden or irregular spread of birds from their normal RANGE; usually as a consequence of a food shortage

IUCN International Union for the Conservation of Nature, responsible for assigning animals and plants to internationally agreed categories of rarity (see table below)

Juvenile young bird that has not reached breeding age

Keel deep extension to the BREASTBONE or STERNUM of a bird to which flight muscles are anchored; absent from many FLIGHTLESS BIRDS

Kleptoparasitism stealing food gathered from other birds; a speciality of skuas and frigatebirds

Lamellae comblike structures used for filtering organisms out of water

Lek display ground where two or more male birds gather to attract females. See DISPLAY.

Life cycle cycle from egg, through CHICK and IMMATURE to ADULT, and then to egg again

Mallee scrub small, scrubby eucalyptus that covers large area of dryish country in Australia

Mandible one of the jaws of a bird that make up the BILL

Mantling threat DISPLAY, usually seen in birds of prey, in which a bird stands over prey, ruffles the mantle (neck) FEATHERS, and droops its WINGS slightly; the display is intended to ward off potential food pirates

Marine associated with or living in the sea

Mating act of copulation in which the cloacae of the two sexes touch, and sperm is released from the male; "mating" is also used as a general term for pair-formation

Melanism an excess of black PIGMENT (melanin) in the PLUMAGE

Migration the movement of animals from one part of the world to another at different times of year to reach food or find a place to breed

Mimicry imitation of one or more characteristics of a SPECIES by another for the gain of the imitator—e.g., vocal mimicry, PLUMAGE mimicry, or egg-coloration mimicry

Mobbing aggressive and often noisy demonstration by one bird against another in order to harass it; often refers to a collective demonstration of small birds against a PREDATOR

Molt replacement of old FEATHERS by new ones

Monogamous taking only a single mate at a time

Monotypic the sole member of a SPECIES' GENUS, FAMILY, ORDER, etc.

Morph a form, usually used to describe a color form when more than one exists

Mutation random changes in genetic material

Mutualism close association between two different organisms from which both benefit

Native belonging to an area; not introduced by humans

Natural selection process whereby individuals with the most appropriate ADAPTATIONS survive to produce offspring

Nest structure built or excavated by a bird or a preexisting site where eggs are laid and remain until they HATCH

Nesting period time from HATCHING to flying. See FLEDGE

Nestling a young bird in the nest

New World the Americas. See OLD WORLD

Niche part of a HABITAT occupied by a SPECIES, defined in terms of all aspects of its lifestyle (e.g., food, competitors, PREDATORS, and other resource requirements)

Nictitating membrane fold of skin, often translucent, which can be drawn across the eye to form a "third eyelid" for protection, lubrication, or cleaning

Nidicolous young birds that remain in the NEST until they can fly. See ALTRICIAL

Nidifugous young birds that leave the NEST soon after HATCHING. See PRECOCIAL

Nocturnal active at night. See DIURNAL

Nomadic wandering; having no fixed home

Oil gland organ located in the rump that secretes an oily substance used in FEATHER care during PREENING; also called uropygial gland or preen gland

Old World non-American continents. See New WORLD

Omnivore animal that eats a wide variety of foods from meat to plants

Opportunistic animal that varies its diet according to what is available

Order level of taxonomic ranking. See CLASS

Ornithologist scientist who specifically studies birds

IUCN CATEGORIES

EX Extinct, when there is no reasonable doubt that the last individual of a species has died.

EW Extinct in the Wild, when a species is known only to survive in captivity or as a naturalized population well outside the past range.

CR Critically Endangered, when a species is facing an extremely high risk of extinction in the wild in the immediate future.

EN Endangered, when a species faces a very high risk of extinction in the wild in the near future.

VU Vulnerable, when a species faces a high risk of extinction in the wild in the medium-term future.

LR Lower Risk, when a species has been evaluated and does not satisfy the criteria for CR, EN, or VU.

DD Data Deficient, when there is not enough information about a species to assess the risk of extinction.

NE Not Evaluated, species that have not been assessed by the IUCN criteria.

Pair-bond behavior that keeps a MATED pair together

Pampas grassy plains (of South America)

Pamprodactyl having all four toes directed forward or having the capability of being so directed

Parallel evolution development of similarities in separate, but related, evolutionary lineages through the operation of similar selective factors

Parasite bird laying its eggs in the nests of other SPECIES and leaving the foster parents to raise the young. See BROOD PARASITISM

Passerine strictly "sparrowlike," but normally used as a shortened form of Passeriformes, the largest ORDER of birds

Pecking order See HIERARCHY

Pellet compact mass of indigestible portions of a bird's food, such as FEATHERS, hair, bone, and scales, that is ejected through the mouth rather than as feces

Pigment substance that gives color to eggs and FEATHERS

Plankton layer of (usually) minute organisms that float near the surface of the ocean or in the air at a certain level above ground

Plumage all the FEATHERS and DOWN that cover a bird

Polyandry when a female mates with several males

Polygamy when a male mates with several females

Polygynous when a male mates with several females in one BREEDING SEASON

Polymorphic when a SPECIES occurs in two or more different forms (usually relating to color). See DIMORPHIC, MORPH

Population distinct group of animals of the same SPECIES or all the animals of that species

Prairie North American STEPPE grassland between 30° N and 55° N

Precocial young birds that leave the NEST after HATCHING. See ALTRICIAL

Predation the act of taking animals by a PREDATOR

Predator animal that kills live prey for food

Preening the act of arranging, cleaning, and otherwise maintaining the PLUMAGE using the BILL; often oil from the OIL GLAND is smeared over the plumage during this process

Prenuptial prior to breeding

Primary feather one of the large FEATHERS of the outer WING. See SECONDARY FEATHER

Promiscuous describes SPECIES in which the sexes come together for mating only and do not form lasting PAIR-BONDS

Quartering the act of flying back and forth over an area, searching it thoroughly

Race See SUBSPECIES

Rain forest TROPICAL and SUBTROPICAL forest with abundant and year-round rainfall; typically SPECIES rich and diverse

Range geographical area over which an organism is distributed

Raptor a bird of prey, usually one belonging to the ORDER Falconiformes

Ratites members of four orders of FLIGHTLESS BIRDS (ostrich, rheas, emus and cassowaries, kiwis) that lack a KEEL on the BREASTBONE

Regurgitation ejection of partly digested food (or the indigestible remains of food in a PELLET) from a bird's GIZZARD

Resident animal that stays in one area all the year around

Roost place where birds sleep

Salt gland part of the excretory system, helping eliminate excess salt, especially in seabirds

Savanna term loosely used to describe open grasslands with scattered trees and bushes, usually in warm areas

Scrape (or hollow) NEST without any nesting material where a shallow depression has been formed to hold the eggs

Scrub vegetation dominated by shrubs (woody plants usually with more than one stem); naturally occurs most often on the arid side of forest or grassland, but often artificially created by humans as a result of DEFORESTATION

Secondary feather one of the large FLIGHT FEATHERS on the inner WING

Sedentary nonmigrating. See RESIDENT

Semiarid describes a region or HABITAT that suffers from lack of water for much of the year, but less dry than a desert

Sequential molt situation in which FEATHERS (usually the WING FEATHERS) are MOLTED in order, as opposed to all at once

Siblings brothers and sisters

Simultaneous polyandry when a female MATES with two or more males and lays CLUTCHES of eggs for each to INCUBATE at the same time

Soaring gliding flight without wingbeats, typically with WINGS widespread, on currents of rising air or on wind currents sweeping upward over steep slopes or waves

Solitary living alone or undertaking tasks alone

Song series of sounds (vocalization), often composed of several or many phrases constructed of repeated elements; normally used by a male to claim a territory and attract a mate

Song flight special flight performance during which territorial SONG is produced; typical of birds occupying open HABITATS with few perches

Specialist animal whose lifestyle involves highly specialized strategems—e.g., feeding with one technique on a particular food

Species a POPULATION or series of populations that interbreed freely, but not with those of other species. See CLASS

Speculum distinctively colored group of FLIGHT FEATHERS

Spur sharp projection on the leg of some game birds; often more developed in males and used in fighting; also found on the carpal joint of some other birds

Steppe open, grassy plains, with few trees or bushes, of the central temperate zone of Eurasia or North America (PRAIRIES), characterized by low and sporadic rainfall and a wide annual temperature variation. "Cold" steppe: temperatures drop well below freezing point in winter, with rainfall concentrated in the summer or evenly distributed throughout the year; "hot" steppe: winter temperatures are higher and rainfall concentrated in winter months

Sternum See BREASTBONE

Stooping dropping rapidly from the air (usually by a RAPTOR in pursuit of prey)

Subadult no longer JUVENILE but not yet fully ADULT

Subarctic region close to the ARCTIC circle, or at high altitude, sharing many of the characteristics of an arctic environment

Suborder subdivision of an ORDER. See CLASS

Sub-Saharan all parts of Africa lying south of the Sahara Desert

Subspecies subdivision of a SPECIES that is distinguishable from the rest of that species; often called a RACE

Subtropics area just outside the TROPICS (i.e., at higher latitudes)

Successive polyandry when one female mates with two or more males during one BREEDING SEASON, producing separate CLUTCHES of eggs one at a time

Sunbathing spreading WINGS and tail and ruffling FEATHERS to expose skin and DOWN feathers to the sun; probably to assist the production of vitamins or to help remove PARASITES

Superspecies two or more SPECIES, geographically separated, of such close relationship that they form a single entity across their combined RANGES

Symbiosis when two or more SPECIES live together for their mutual benefit more successfully than either could live on its own

Syndactyl foot having two toes joined for part of their length

Syrinx vocal organ unique to birds at the division of the trachea

Tactolocation method of sensing, often to locate prey, by using touch

Taiga belt of coniferous forests (evergreen conifers such as firs, pines, and spruces) lying below the latitude of TUNDRA

Tail streamer specially elongated tail FEATHER (e.g., as seen on a swallow, tern, or tropicbird)

Talon sharp, hooked CLAWS used for grabbing, holding, and killing prey (usually refers to those of PREDATORS such as birds of prey and owls)

Temperate zone zones between latitudes 40° and 60° where the climate is variable or seasonal

Terrestrial living on land

Territorial defending an area; in birds usually refers to a bird or birds that exclude others of the same SPECIES from their living area and in which they will usually nest

Territory area that an animal or animals consider their own and defend against intruders

Thermal an area of (warm) air that rises by convection

Trachea See WINDPIPE

Tree hole any crevice or hollow in the trunk or limbs of a tree that can be used by birds for ROOSTING or NESTING

Tribe term sometimes used to group certain SPECIES or GENERA within a FAMILY. See CLASS

Tropics geographical area lying between 22.5° N and 22.5° S

Tundra open grassy or shrub-covered lands of the far north

Upending swiveling motion used by swimming WILDFOWL, immersing the head and foreparts of the body to reach submerged food

Vagrant individual bird blown off course or having migrated abnormally to reach a geographical area where its SPECIES is not normally found

Variety occasional variation in a SPECIES, not sufficiently persistent or geographically separated to form a SUBSPECIES

Vertebrate animal with a backbone (e.g., fish, amphibian, bird, or mammal)

Wader term sometimes used for "shorebird," including sandpipers, plovers, and related SPECIES; neither term is strictly accurate, since some species live neither on the shore nor by water

Wattle fleshy protuberance, usually near the base of the BILL

Wetland freshwater or saltwater marshes

Wildfowl inclusive term for geese, ducks, and swans

Windpipe tube that takes air from the mouth and nostrils to the lungs; also called the trachea

Wing the forelimb; the primary means of flight in flying birds, carrying the SECONDARY and PRIMARY FEATHERS (quills) and their smaller COVERTS

Wing patch well-defined area of color or pattern on the WING (usually the upper wing) of a bird

Wingspan measurement from tip to tip of the spread WINGS

Wing spur sharp projection at or near the bend of the WING. See SPUR

Wintering ground area where a migrant spends the nonbreeding season

Wishbone the furcula, formed by the two clavicles, or collar bones, joining the shoulders across the forepart of the STERNUM

Zygodactyl having two toes directed forward and two backward

Further Reading

General

Attenborough, D., *The Life of Birds*, BBC Books, London, U.K., 1998

Brooke, M., and Birkhead, T., *The Cambridge Encyclopedia of Ornithology*, Cambridge University Press, Cambridge, U.K., 1991

Chatterjee, S., *The Rise of Birds: 225 Million Years of Evolution*, The Johns Hopkins University Press, Baltimore, MD, 1997

Clements, J. F., *Birds of the World: A Checklist*, Ibis, Vista, CA, 2000

del Hoyo, J., Elliott, A., and Sargatal, J. (eds.), *The Handbook of the Birds of the World*, Vols. 1–7, Lynx Edicions, Barcelona, Spain, 1992–2002 (Vols. 8–16 in preparation)

Ehrlich, P. R., Dobkin, D. S., and Wheye, D., *The Birder's Handbook*, Simon & Schuster Inc., New York, NY, 1988

Elphick, C., Dunning, J. B. Jr., and Sibley, D., *The Sibley Guide to Bird Life and Behavior*, Alfred A. Knopf, New York, NY, 2001

Elphick, J. (ed.), *The Random House Atlas of Bird Migration*, Random House, New York, NY, 1995

Feduccia, A., *The Origin and Evolution of Birds*, Yale University Press, New Haven, CT, 1996

Gill, F., and Poole, A. (eds.), *The Birds of North America: Species Accounts*, American Ornithologists' Union, Washington, DC, 1992

Howard, R., and Moore, A., *A Complete Checklist of the Birds of the World* (2nd edn.), Academic Press, New York, NY, 1980

Jonsson, L., *Birds of Europe, with North Africa and the Middle East*, Helm, London, U.K., 1992

Kaplan, G., and Rogers, L. J., *Birds: Their Habits and Skills*, Allen & Unwin, Crows Nest, New South Wales, Australia, 2001

Marchant, S., and Higgins, P. J., *Handbook of Australian, New Zealand and Antarctic Birds*, Oxford University Press, Melbourne, Australia, 1990

Monroe, B. L., and Sibley, C. G., *A World Checklist of Birds*, Yale University Press, New Haven, CT, 1993

Page, J., and Morton, E.S., *Lords of the Air: The Smithsonian Book of Birds*, Smithsonian Institution Press, Washington, DC, 1989

Perrins, C. M., and Middleton, A., *The Encyclopedia of Birds*, Facts on File, New York, NY, 1997

Perrins, C. M., *Firefly Encyclopedia of Birds*, Firefly Books, Buffalo and Toronto, Canada, 2003

Poole, A. F., Stettenheim, P., and Gill, F. B., *The Birds of North America*, American Ornithologists' Union/Academy of Natural Sciences, Philadelphia, PA, 1992–present

Sibley, D., *North American Bird Guide*, Alfred A. Knopf, New York, NY, 2000

Snow, D. W., and Perrins, C. M., *Birds of the Western Palearctic* (concise edn.), Oxford University Press, Oxford, U.K./New York, NY, 1998

Sziij, L., *Welty's Life of Birds* (5th edn.), Academic Press, St. Louis, MO, 2003

Specific to this volume

Ali, S., *Handbook of the Birds of India and Pakistan*, Oxford University Press, Delhi, India, 1978

Brown, L. H., Urban, E. K., and Newman, K., *The Birds of Africa*, Vols. 1–6, Academic Press, London, U.K., 1982

Johnsgard, P. A., *Bustards, Hemipodes and Sandgrouse: Birds of Dry Places*, Oxford University Press, Oxford, UK., 1991

Johnsgard, P. A., *The Grouse of the World*, Croom Helm, London, U.K., 1983

Johnsgard, P. A., *The Quails, Partridges and Francolins of the World*, Oxford University Press, Oxford, U.K., 1988

Johnsgard, P. A., *The Pheasants of the World*, Smithsonian Institution Press, Washington, DC, 1999

Madge, S., and McGowan, P., *Pheasants, Partridges, and Grouse*, Princeton University Press, Princeton, NJ, 2002

Useful Websites

General

http://www.aou.org
Founded in 1883, the American Ornithologists' Union is the oldest and largest organization in the New World devoted to the scientific study of birds

http://www.audubon.org
The website of the National Audubon Society includes news, avian science, product reports, and conservation work throughout America

http://www.birdlife.net
Website of the worldwide BirdLife International partnership, leading to partner organizations around the globe and to information about species

http://www.birds.cornell/edu
Cornell Laboratory of Ornithology website, leading to information about North American birds and actions you can take to study and conserve them

http://www.bsc-eoc.org/links
"Bird Links to the world" leads you to websites for many countries, detailing sites, species, books, and other information on the birds in each region

http://www.fatbirder.com
Fat Birder is a superb portal to 15,000 birding website links and has a page for every country in the world and all U.S., Canadian, and Australian states and provinces

http://www.surfbirds.com
A joint American-British website that includes breaking bird news items, articles of interest, rare bird reports, identification features, and more

Specific to this volume

http://www.pheasant.org.uk
The central site for the World Pheasant Association, dealing with many critically endangered species

http://www.western.edu/bio/young/gunnsg/gunnsg.htm
An excellent site about sage grouse, with useful links to other sites

Picture Credits

Abbreviations A Ardea London; BCC Bruce Coleman Collection; FLPA Frank Lane Picture Agency; NHPA Natural History Photographic Agency; NPL naturepl.com; OSF Oxford Scientific Films; t = top; b = bottom; c = center; l = left; r = right

Jacket tl Stan Osolinski/OSF; tr Martin Harvey/NHPA; bl Haroldo Palo Jr./NHPA; br N.W. Harwood/Aquila; 10–11 Hans & Judy Beste/A; 12 Karl Ammann/NPL; 14–15 Chris Knights/A; 17 Martyn Chillmaid/OSF; 18 Konrad Wothe/OSF; 19 Robin Bush/OSF; 20–21 Fred Bruemmer/BCC; 22–23 Tony Heald/NPL; 24 Fred Bruemmer/BCC; 25 Vincent Munier/NPL; 26–27 Jen & Des Bartlett/Survival Anglia/OSF; 27 Jean-Paul Ferrero/A; 28 Stan Osolinski/OSF; 29 Jean-Paul Ferrero/A; 31 Clive Bromhall/OSF; 32–33 Hans & Judy Beste/Animals Animals/OSF; 34–35 Frank Schneidermeyer/OSF; 36–37 Mark Jones/OSF; 38 A.N.T./NHPA; 39 M. Jones/Minden Pictures/FLPA; 41 P. Morris/A; 41 inset Michael Fogden/OSF; 42–43 François Gohier/A; 45 David Tipling/OSF; 46t Robin Chittenden/FLPA; 46c William S. Clark/FLPA; 47 Steve Turner/OSF; 48 Michael Sewell/OSF; 50–51 John Shaw/NHPA; 52–53 Nigel J. Dennis/NHPA; 54c Joanna Van Gruisen/A; 54b Dr. Eckart Pott/NHPA; 55 Michael Kavanagh/Survival Anglia/OSF; 56–57 Chris Knights/A; 58 Manfred Danegger/NHPA; 59 Allan G. Potts/BCC; 61 Kenneth W. Fink/A; 62 Terry Whittaker/FLPA; 63 G.I. Bernard/OSF; 64 Bob Glover/BCC; 65 Robert Maier/BCC; 66–67 Stephen J. Krasemann/NHPA; 68–69 Chris Knights/A; 69 Mark Hamblin/OSF; 70–71 Tom Vezo/NPL; 72–73 Rich Kirchner/NHPA; 74–75 Daphne Kinzler/FLPA; 77 D. Maslowski/FLPA; 78–79 Ray Richardson/Animals Animals/OSF; 80 S. & D. & K. Maslowski/FLPA; 81 Chris Sharp/OSF; 82–83 Jen & Des Bartlett/Survival Anglia/OSF; 85 Stan Osolinski/OSF; 86–87 Kenneth Day/OSF; 88–89 Carlos Sanchez/OSF; 90 Hellio & Van Ingen/NHPA; 90–91 M. Watson/A; 93 Bert & Babs Wells/OSF; 94–95 Jorg & Petra Wegner/BCC; 96 Jean-Paul Ferrero/A; 96–97 Daniel Heuclin/NHPA; 99 R.M. Bloomfield/A; 101, 102–103 Yossi Eshbol/FLPA; 105c E. McNamara/A; 105b Roger Brown/OSF; 106–107 Jurgen & Christine Sohns/FLPA; 108 Hans & Judy Beste/Animals Animals/OSF; 110–111 Bert & Babs Wells/OSF

Artists **Norman Arlott, Denys Ovenden, and Ad Cameron** with Trevor Boyer, Robert Gillmor, Peter Harrison, Sean Milne, and Ian Willis

Set Index

A **bold** number shows the volume and is followed by the relevant page numbers (eg., **15:** 8, 38).

Common names in **bold** (e.g., **bateleur**) mean that the bird has an illustrated main entry in the set. Underlined page numbers (e.g., **15:** 36–37) refer to the main entry for that bird.

Italic page numbers (e.g., **20:** 49) point to illustrations of birds in parts of the set other than the main entry.

Page numbers in parentheses—e.g., **18:** (34)—locate information in At-a-glance boxes.

Birds with main entries in the set are indexed under their common names, alternative common names, and scientific names.